Tiberius Caesar

IN THE SAME SERIES

General Editors: Eric J. Evans and P. D. King

LANCASTER PAMPHLETS

Tiberius Caesar

David Shotter

London and New York

First published 1992
by Routledge
11 New Fetter Lane, London EC4P 4EE

Simultaneously published in the USA and Canada
by Routledge
a division of Routledge, Chapman and Hall, Inc.
29 West 35th Street, New York, NY 10001

Typeset in 10/12pt Bembo by
Ponting–Green Publishing Services, Sunninghill, Berks
Printed in Great Britain by
Clays Ltd, St Ives plc

British Library Cataloguing in Publication Data
Shotter, David
Tiberius Caesar. – (Lancaster Pamphlets Series)
I. Title II. Series
937.07092

Library of Congress Cataloging in Publication Data
Shotter, D. C. A. (David Colin Arthur)
Tiberius Caesar / David Shotter.
p.   cm. – (Lancaster pamphlets)
Includes bibliographical references
1. Tiberius, Emperor of Rome, 42 B.C.–37 A.D.
2. Rome–History–Tiberius, 14–37. 3. Roman emperors–
Biography. I. Title.
II. Series.
DG282.S46   1992
937'.07'092–dc20
[B]   92-13934

ISBN 0–415–07654–4

Contents

Appendices

Foreword

Lancaster Pamphlets offer concise and up-to-date accounts of major historical topics, primarily for the help of students preparing for Advanced Level examinations, though they should also be of value to those pursuing introductory courses in universities and other institutions of higher education. Without being all-embracing, their aims are to bring some of the central themes or problems confronting students and teachers into sharper focus than the textbook writer can hope to do; to provide the reader with some of the results of recent research which the textbook may not embody; and to stimulate thought about the whole interpretation of the topic under discussion.

Figures

Acknowledgements

My thanks are due to Mr Peter Lee of the Lancaster University Archaeology Unit, who prepared the maps which appear as Figures 4 and 5; also to Mrs June Cross and Miss Susan Waddington of the History Department at Lancaster University for the preparation of the manuscript.

1

Introduction

Tiberius Caesar was an enigma to his contemporaries; subsequent generations found this taciturn and reclusive figure no easier to fathom. When in AD 14, at the age of 56, he succeeded Augustus as *princeps*, he was a man of considerable – mostly military – experience; yet despite this, there were serious anxieties as to whether his character really suited him to the demands of the job, anxieties which he himself appears in some measure to have shared. Some felt that Augustus had adopted him as his successor either because there was no satisfactory alternative or even so that a poor successor would shed a particularly favourable light on his own memory. To many, Tiberius' reserved nature concealed haughtiness and arrogance, perhaps even a tendency to cruelty and perversion.

Once in power, Tiberius expressed reluctance to exercise the responsibilities and take the opportunities which it offered. Had he been unwillingly projected to prominence by events or by the machinations of his scheming mother, Livia Drusilla? Or was it due to the backing of members of the senatorial nobility who thought they recognised in Tiberius a man of 'republican' sentiments, who would restore to them the kinds of privileges their families had enjoyed in the old republic? Indeed, Tiberius' early actions and pronouncements as *princeps* seemed to suggest that he might perform such a role and that he believed the

Augustan *respublica* to represent too sharp a departure from the traditions of the past.

Part of the enigma lay in the fact that such sentiments were genuinely felt by Tiberius; yet at the same time he had an inordinate reverence for Augustus, his achievements and his form of government, despite the fact that prior to AD 14 Tiberius' life had been dominated to the point of near-destruction by adherence to Augustus' wishes and requirements. Such, however, was the self-effacement of the new *princeps* that not only did he express distaste for the trappings of power but he would not even willingly accept the name Augustus on the grounds of his unworthiness to hold it.

A further element of the enigma of Tiberius Caesar was the fact that, despite such sentiments, his reign did not in fact mark any kind of reversion to the practices of the old republic. On the contrary, it eventually represented a descent into tyranny, in which Tiberius came under the influence of the unscrupulous prefect of the praetorian guard, Lucius Aelius Sejanus, and was persuaded to live out a bitter and frustrated retirement in isolation, much of it spent on the island of Capreae (Capri), whilst Rome and its politics were dominated first by Sejanus himself and subsequently by his equally corrupt successor, Sertorius Macro.

How did Tiberius fall under the malicious influence of such men? Why was his dependence on them not prevented by the influence and support of members of his own family or of his long-standing friends? There is again an apparently baffling inconsistency in the fact that a man who rarely shared confidences could fall under such totally dominating influences. Frustration at this inconsistency was keenly felt by Tiberius' contemporaries. 'What hope is there for the young Caligula, if even Tiberius with all his experience has been deranged by his exercise of supreme power?' was the pertinent question posed by the respected Tiberian senator, Lucius Arruntius, who committed suicide shortly before Tiberius' own death.

The purpose of the present work is to examine the life and career of Tiberius Caesar and to illuminate the influences upon him; it will also highlight Tiberius' own ideas on government and the reasons for the ultimate frustration and failure. Indeed, it will seek to answer questions which in all probability oppressed Tiberius as he increasingly immersed himself in the occult towards the end of his life.

Much of the controversy which over the years has surrounded the life and principate of Tiberius has derived from differing interpretations of the contemporary and later classical sources; for this reason, especial attention will be paid to these writers in an attempt to clarify their views of Tiberius Caesar. One thing, however, is certain: the good reputation with his own and subsequent generations which at one stage he stated as his ultimate ambition eluded him, and the accolade of posthumous deification, granted readily enough to his predecessor, was denied to him.

2
Tiberius' early life

Tiberius Claudius Nero, later to become Tiberius Caesar, was born on 16 November, 42 BC; this was the year which saw Octavian and Marc Antony inflict defeat upon Brutus and Cassius, thus finally avenging the murder of Julius Caesar two years previously. As a member of the Claudian family (*gens Claudia*), Tiberius could look back to a long line of famous, often brilliantly talented, ancestors. Few generations of the Roman republic had not seen a Claudian exercising a dominant or maverick role; they were a family firmly at the centre of the network of aristocratic patronage which had been the life-blood of the *respublica*. Tiberius' parents were in fact both Claudians, though from different branches of the family. His father was, like Tiberius himself, called Tiberius Claudius Nero; his branch of the family was comparatively undistinguished. Some members had been active at the time of the Punic wars in the third century BC; more recently, only Tiberius' paternal grandfather, also called Tiberius Claudius Nero, appears to have played an active role in politics (see Figure 1).

Tiberius' mother was Livia Drusilla; she derived her name from another influential republican family, the Livii Drusi. However, her father was a Claudius Pulcher who had been adopted in infancy by Marcus Livius Drusus, a tribune in 91 BC. Under the terms of adoption, Livia's father took the name of Marcus Livius Drusus Claudianus. He played an active part in

4

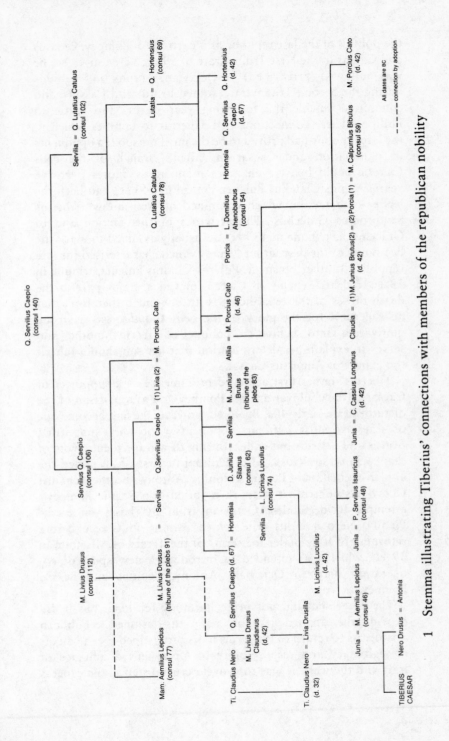

1 Stemma illustrating Tiberius' connections with members of the republican nobility

the politics of the late republic as a partisan of Pompey, Crassus and Caesar in the First Triumvirate of 59 BC. Later, in 43 BC, he was outlawed (proscribed) by Octavian, Antony and Lepidus during the Second Triumvirate, joined Brutus and Cassius, and committed suicide the following year during the battle of Philippi. These connections tied Tiberius to families which in the late republic had proved to be the most outspoken opponents of domination and Caesarism. Livia's branch of the *gens Claudia* could boast even more momentous figures over the years: Appius Claudius Pulcher, consul in 143 BC, had been the leader of a faction which contained his son-in-law, Tiberius Sempronius Gracchus. The activities of this faction and of Gracchus as tribune in 133 BC are usually assumed to mark the beginning of the descent into chaos which characterised the late republic. Another kinsman, Publius Clodius Pulcher, tribune in 58 BC and arch-enemy of Cicero, played a major part in the death throes of the republic. It is little wonder, therefore, that an eagerness for the glory of the *gens Claudia* was a strong motivating factor behind the conduct of Tiberius' mother and serves to explain her determination that her son should inherit the mantle of Augustus Caesar.

Tiberius' father first achieved prominence as a supporter of Caesar in the civil war against Pompey and as a partisan of the dictator in the early 40s. By 44 BC, however, he had become one of Caesar's most extreme opponents, not only supporting Brutus and Cassius but endeavouring to win for them a vote of thanks as tyrannicides. After Philippi he first of all joined the abortive rebellion of Lucius Antonius (Antony's brother) against Octavian's control of Italy, then (briefly) in Sextus Pompey's attempts to destabilise Octavian from his bases on Sicily. Finally, Nero and his wife joined Antony in Greece before returning to Italy under the terms of the Treaty of Misenum in 39 BC, which was intended to introduce a new spirit of co-operation between Octavian, Antony, Lepidus and Sextus Pompey.

The agreement did not bring harmony for long, but it did provide the opportunity for many disillusioned republican aristocrats to return to Italy; this in its turn helped to lend an air of legitimacy and respectability to Octavian's dominance of Italy and the west. It was to prove a crucial step in the process of establishing Octavian and his faction as the true defenders of liberty and the republic.

Even more important, both politically and personally, was Octavian's decision to divorce his wife, Scribonia, and facilitate a divorce between Tiberius Nero and Livia. Despite the fact that Livia was pregnant with her second son, Octavian ignored the moral and religious objections and married her. This marriage served to bind Octavian with the core of the republican nobility, and provided a social respectability which was lacking in his own more humble origins. It was probably the most important decision of Octavian's life, and the marriage was one of the most influential in the history of Rome. Livia's sons were now the stepsons of the man who would soon rule the Roman world as Augustus Caesar.

Tiberius and his brother, Nero Drusus, were brought up in Octavian's household as his stepsons, although Tiberius at least maintained a contact with his father – to the extent that it was natural for him to pronounce his father's funeral eulogy in 32 BC, still only 9 years old. It cannot reasonably be expected that these domestic and political upheavals failed to leave their mark on the young Tiberius Nero, and they may well help to explain the great desire for stability that was to be so prominent a feature of Tiberius' aspirations as *princeps*.

Tiberius' development from childhood to manhood occurred during a crucial period for the *respublica*, which saw the inexorable progress towards the battle of Actium in 31 BC and the subsequent establishment of the Augustan principate. It is evident from his own accession as *princeps* in AD 14 that Tiberius found no difficulty in reconciling the ideas of the traditional *respublica* and the special commission entrusted to Augustus to restore and stabilise it. Augustus' massive prestige (*auctoritas*), which derived from his leadership of the Caesarian faction, from his victory at Actium, and from his reconciliation with the descendants of the republican nobility, made him the natural person to save the republic from what had seemed for most of the first century BC its inevitable disintegration. The young Tiberius was associated with the new order of things as he took part prominently in the victory parades that followed Actium.

It was not long before Augustus began his protracted and chequered search for a successor to his power and position, the complexities of which are documented in the stemma which appears as Figure 2. A major purpose was to weld together a faction of disparate elements – family, republican nobility, and 'new men' who had risen in his service in the years between Caesar's murder and the battle of Actium. The primacy of this faction, however, he determined should reside within his own family, the *Julii*; it was for the same principle that he had decided in 44–43 BC that he, and not Marc Antony, was Caesar's true political heir.

The first clear indication of this was the marriage in 25 BC between his daughter, Julia, and his sister's son, Gaius Marcellus. Marcellus, however, did not live to become Augustus' heir; his death in 22 BC probably avoided a deepening of the offence caused to Augustus' old and trusted friend, Marcus Agrippa, who in all likelihood saw his marginalisation by the young Marcellus as poor reward for his contribution to the stability of Augustus' present position. The alienation of Agrippa may, however, have threatened a larger crisis than is sometimes supposed; for to counter it Augustus drew him into the family as Julia's new husband, and it may have been at about this time that Tiberius became the husband of Agrippa's daughter, Vipsania Agrippina – a marriage which proved to be perhaps the happiest and most rewarding feature of Tiberius' whole life.

Augustus' purpose in these arrangements was to secure strength for the *Julii*, by binding into the family powerful – but potentially destructive – elements. The *princeps* did not, however, envisage that factional succession would pass to Agrippa or Tiberius, important though they were as workers for the regime. The inheritors were to be the sons that Augustus hoped would be produced by the marriage of Agrippa and Julia. When his hope was fulfilled, the *princeps* showed his intention by straightaway adopting the two eldest boys as his own sons. They are known to us by their adopted names of Gaius Julius Caesar and Lucius Julius Caesar.

None of this appears to have caused Tiberius any problems. As the stepson of Augustus, Tiberius' role appears to have been firmly rooted in the service of the *princeps*. In the late 20s BC, he was fully involved in the diplomatic and military activities which led to the recovery from the Parthians of the legionary standards lost by Crassus in 53 BC and by Decidius Saxa in 36 BC. By this success, Roman pride in the east was salvaged and

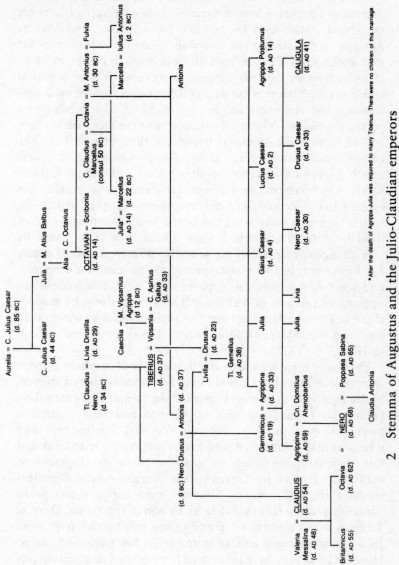

2 Stemma of Augustus and the Julio-Claudian emperors

Aurelia = C. Julius Caesar (d. 85 BC)

C. Julius Caesar (d. 44 BC)

Julia = M. Atius Balbus

Atia = C. Octavius

OCTAVIAN = Scribonia (d. AD 14)

Julia* = Marcellus (d. AD 14) (d. 22 BC)

C. Claudius Marcellus (consul 50 BC) = Octavia = M. Antonius = Fulvia (d. 30 BC)

Marcella = Iullus Antonius (d. 2 BC)

Antonia

Tl. Claudius = Livia Drusilla Nero (d. AD 29) (d. 34 BC)

Caecilia = M. Vipsanius Agrippa (d 12 BC)

TIBERIUS = Vipsania = C. Asinius Gallus (d. AD 37) (d. AD 33)

(d. 9 BC) Nero Drusus = Antonia (d. AD 37)

Livilla = Drusus (d. AD 23)

Tl. Gemellus (d. AD 38)

Julia

Julia

Livia

Julia

Gaius Caesar (d. AD 4)

Lucius Caesar (d. AD 2)

Agrippa Postumus (d. AD 14)

Nero Caesar (d. AD 30)

Drusus Caesar (d. AD 33)

CALIGULA (d. AD 41)

Germanicus = Agrippina (d. AD 19) (d. AD 33)

Agrippina (d. AD 59) = NERO (d. AD 68) = Poppaea Sabina (d. AD 65)

Claudia Antonia

Cn. Domitius Ahenobarbus

Valeria Messalina (d. AD 48) = CLAUDIUS (d. AD 54) = Octavia (d. AD 62)

Britannicus (d. AD 55)

*After the death of Agrippa Julia was required to marry Tiberius. There were no children of this marriage.

Rome's superiority over Armenia and Parthia established.

From then until 7 BC, it was the battlefields of Europe that exercised Tiberius – first in Gaul and then as part of a 'triple spearhead' along with his brother, Nero Drusus, and Marcus Agrippa in the attempt to establish Roman sovereignty as far east as the River Elbe, as part of the scheme to create an Elbe–Danube frontier for the Empire in Europe. It was a period which marked Tiberius out as an efficient commander, yet a self-effacing and retiring man. It was evidently also a satisfying period that allowed Tiberius to enjoy close contact with his men and to form associations of friendship that were to last. The comradeship of the battlefield is well conveyed in the nickname which Suetonius ascribes to this period – Biberius Caldius Mero, which referred to Tiberius' reputation as a drinker. It is evident that Tiberius liked the 'anonymity' of the battlefields, which kept him away from the brittle and dangerous world of dynastic politics and which gave him a context in which he was confident of performing soundly. Widely popular he may not have been, but he was respected for his cautious efficiency and achievement. It is also apparent that when Tiberius did not approve of the way in which a job was being done, he made it clear; one enemy deriving from this period, and who was to bear a grudge, was Marcus Lollius, whom Tiberius replaced in Gaul in 16 BC.

Physically remote though the battlefields of northern Europe were, domestic politics could never be far away from a stepson of the *princeps*. Augustus' hopes for the future were centred on Gaius and Lucius, the sons of Agrippa and Julia. Agrippa's premature death in 12 BC not only deprived Tiberius of a man who was his father-in-law and his friend, it also left Gaius and Lucius without a father to supervise their development to manhood. It was to Tiberius that Augustus turned at this moment of need, despite Tiberius' own happy marriage to Vipsania and the fact that they had a son of their own, Drusus. Tiberius was required to abandon his family and step in as Julia's new husband and as guardian of her two young sons. How far Livia may have influenced her husband in adopting this course is not clear, but she may have seen her son's marriage to the widowed daughter of the *princeps* as the most effective way of promoting the glory of the *gens Claudia*. For Tiberius, the change was a disaster; not only did he give up the family he

10

loved, but before long he was recalled from Germany to take his place in the political arena in Rome. This brought him face to face with the reality of the sacrifice he had been called upon to make. According to Suetonius, he once followed Vipsania in the street, trying to talk to her; Augustus made sure that this did not happen again. Like Agrippa before him he had no alternative but to bear the insult to his pride contained in Julia's promiscuity; in addition, it appears from the account of Dio Cassius (*Roman History*, LV.9) that he did not enjoy a good relationship with his stepsons.

Despite his elevation to a second consulship in 7 BC and Augustus' decision to confer upon him the following year a grant of the tribunician power, which effectively marked out Tiberius as having achieved the standing of Agrippa, Tiberius decided in 6 BC to turn his back on everything and retire to the island of Rhodes – alone apart from a few friends and the company of an astrologer, named Thrasyllus, who was to exercise a considerable influence over Tiberius in later years. It is evident that Rome was taken by surprise by Tiberius' retirement; indeed Augustus evidently regarded it as desertion and dereliction of duty. Tiberius at the time explained his decision as due to his own fatigue and to the status of his stepsons and his wish not to impede their progress; many, however, thought that the real reason lay in his unhappiness at his wife's behaviour. More recently, a psychiatric study of Tiberius has regarded this 'island psychology' as an expression of his feelings about his own inadequacy and inability to relate to people. It is evident that his close relationships were few in number, yet he committed himself deeply on those few occasions; not only was his relationship with Vipsania an example, but so too was his devotion to his brother, Nero Drusus. Following the latter's death in Germany in 9 BC, Tiberius had accompanied the cortège all the way to Rome on foot. As emperor, Tiberius' unquestioning allegiance to Sejanus provides another example of such a commitment.

Even on Rhodes, however, Tiberius could not escape from domestic politics; Augustus' anger soon turned Tiberius' retirement into an enforced exile, and it was clearly 'fashionable' amongst Augustus' associates to regard Tiberius with contempt. One of them, Tiberius' old enemy, Marcus Lollius, now elevated to the role of companion (*comes*) to Gaius Caesar, offered at a dinner party to go to Rhodes and bring back the exile's head. Another particularly personal reminder of his changing fortunes came with the nearby presence, as proconsul of Asia (within whose 'jurisdiction' the island of Rhodes fell), of Gaius Asinius Gallus, the son of the historian Pollio. Gallus had married Vipsania and was trying to adopt Drusus as his son. Until Gallus' death in AD 33 the bitter hostility between himself and Tiberius was barely concealed.

In 2 BC Augustus seems finally to have become aware of his daughter's waywardness; he acted against her in the harshest way open to the father of an adulterous daughter, punishing her with exile and ignoring Tiberius' distant attempts to intercede on behalf of a wife for whom he can have had little regard. In requiring a divorce between Tiberius and Julia, Augustus was of course severing a significant link between himself and Tiberius, which would have left Tiberius more than ever dependent for his survival upon his mother's influence with Augustus.

Again, however, fortune was to intervene decisively in the plans of both Augustus and Tiberius. Despite the eclipse of Julia, the career progress of her sons was unimpeded; offices and honours were bestowed upon them and the future primacy of Augustus' faction seemed assured. Yet by AD 4 both were dead, apparently innocently, though some saw the involvement of Livia who was concerned to protect and advance her son. After Lucius' death in AD 2, Augustus allowed Tiberius to return to Rome, though on the understanding that this was not to mean a return to politics. Following the death of Gaius two years later, Augustus' options were much reduced, and it may well be that Livia and some elements of the older senatorial nobility sought to take advantage – evidently to check the rise of the new senatorial families whose progress Augustus had fostered.

These older elements of the nobility possibly saw in Tiberius a potential champion – because of the antiquity of his own family so deeply rooted in the republican past. Dio Cassius relates amongst the events of AD 4 a long discussion between Augustus and Livia on the subject of the fate of one Cnaeus Cornelius Cinna Magnus, a descendant of Pompey whose name was naturally associated with the republic's cause against Caesar. The outcome of this discussion was the awarding to

12

Cinna of a consulship for AD 5. Although no specific connection is made between this event and the shift in dynastic policies in AD 4, it is difficult not to assume that Augustus in his moment of dynastic weakness had been put under pressure by the old nobility.

It is clear that in his dynastic reconstruction in AD 4 Augustus could have continued to ignore Tiberius in favour of Agrippa Postumus, the last surviving son of Agrippa and Julia, and Germanicus, Tiberius' nephew who was married to Agrippina, a daughter of Agrippa and Julia. Tradition says that Augustus would have liked to place his hopes fairly and squarely on Germanicus' shoulders. Instead, he created a more complex dynastic 'package'. Tiberius and Agrippa Postumus were formally to be adopted as Augustus' sons; officially Tiberius would now be known as Tiberius Julius Caesar. Tiberius himself was required to adopt Germanicus as his son and heir, ignoring the expectations of his own son, Drusus.

Augustus had therefore compromised; realising the power of Livia, Tiberius and the older nobility, he had acknowledged their force as a faction. However, he had ensured that although his Julian faction might temporarily have to bear eclipse by the Claudians, it would on the death of Tiberius once again come into its own through Germanicus, Agrippina and their children. Further, should Tiberius once again prove 'unreliable', the dynastic balance could point in two alternative directions – Germanicus or Agrippa Postumus; both of these were by birth or marriage firmly anchored within Augustus' Julian faction.

Thus Tiberius once again emerged into political prominence; however, Augustus, perhaps recognising where Tiberius' real strength lay, committed him for much of the next five years to military projects in Europe. Initially the intention was probably to breathe new life into the dream of an imperial frontier on the Elbe. However, progress towards this was first hampered by the need for Tiberius to go to the Danube between AD 6 and 9, in the wake of the Pannonian rebellion, and then finally destroyed by the loss of Quinctilius Varus and three legions in the great disaster near Osnabrück in AD 9. This dealt the final blow to an Elbe–Danube frontier, and left Augustus and Tiberius having to settle for a European frontier based upon the Rhine and the Danube. It should not, however, be forgotten how close to disaster the Empire had been between AD 6 and 9 and that it was Tiberius' military strength which had saved the day.

Between AD 4 and 14 it is likely that Augustus' ability to govern began to diminish, and that greater responsibility fell on to the shoulders of others. Foremost amongst these was of course Tiberius, and correspondence between Augustus and Tiberius, quoted by Suetonius, indicates the degree of reliance which the *princeps* placed upon his stepson. The fact that Tiberius enjoyed the same powers as Augustus – the proconsular power and the tribunician power – indicates that he was in a position to act for Augustus. Yet others too were important, and rivalries still existed within the imperial family.

Germanicus, for example, for a time read the speeches of the *princeps* to the senate, and after Tiberius' successful stabilising of the Rhine in AD 9 it was to Germanicus that supreme power in that area was given. Not surprisingly, people readily imagined a rivalry between Germanicus and Tiberius, particularly in view of the way in which they had been forced together in the 'package' of AD 4 and the great difference that was perceived in their characters. Comparison between the two probably served to heighten the public perception of Tiberius as reclusive; this remoteness was readily seen as a screen behind which Tiberius practised acts of cruel perversion.

Included too in the 'package' of AD 4 was Agrippa Postumus, though his role is none too clear. Some kind of scandal in AD 7 led to his banishment, along with his sister and the poet, Ovid; it is not clear whether this was political in nature or had anything to do with continuing rivalry between the factions within the imperial family. Livia, however, feared that Tiberius' position could be weakened by the fact that in the last two years of his life Augustus appears to have attempted reconciliation with his grandson; although it is not clear what Augustus intended, some people evidently expected a new twist in the plans for succession.

Despite this, however, in Augustus' last years Tiberius was the most powerful man in the Empire after the *princeps* himself; and with him had risen his own partisans – to the extent that one historian has talked of the Empire being already ruled by a 'government-in-waiting'. However, the real test was still to come; for many people Augustus had taken on a kind of immortality, and it was scarcely possible to imagine Rome and

14

the Empire without him. Indeed, Augustus had himself helped to foster the illusion by portraying himself on the coinage as perpetually youthful.

His death in August AD 14, after forty-five years in power, precipitated a crisis both for the principate and for the man who had guarded it for the previous decade. Could Augustus' personal mantle be passed on? Could Tiberius match up to the *auctoritas* of the late *princeps*? How was power to be transmitted? Amidst so much doubt and diffidence, one person retained a determined ambition: Livia, Augustus' widow and Tiberius' mother, knew that the moment of her family, the Claudians, had come. Significantly, Tacitus shows that in Livia's report of Augustus' death and Tiberius' accession, she stressed that the new man at the centre of affairs was named not Tiberius Julius Caesar (as Tiberius had been known since his adoption in AD 4) but Tiberius Claudius Nero, the head of the *gens Claudia*, and presumed champion of the *respublica*.

The year AD 14 would provide searching tests for the system of Augustus and for its new presumed leader; the traumas of his early life and the crises induced by Augustus' dynastic policy will not have failed to leave scars on the personality of Tiberius Caesar. Not least amongst Tiberius' difficulties was the fact that whilst most people readily acknowledged his military competence, they did not really know him as a political leader and suspected that his eventual emergence at the top had not been managed without a certain amount of suspect or even criminal behaviour. This reputation was significant, and Tiberius himself recognised it as a millstone around his neck. Moreover, whilst he had been on the political scene in one way or another for more than three decades, to most he was still unknown – and therefore an object of both suspicion and fear. In this way, Tiberius carried into his own principate a heavy legacy from his earlier years.

3
The new *princeps*

The previous chapter has made frequent – and unquestioning – references to Augustus' 'dynastic' or 'succession' policy; in the later years of the first century AD, with the benefit of hindsight, Augustus' policy was recognised for what it really was – the establishment of a hereditary monarchy, built around the Julian and Claudian families. As we have seen, it was Augustus' earliest hope that the former – his own family – would predominate. Augustus knew, however, that it would have been self-defeating to have proclaimed such an intention openly. He had come to power as a faction leader; despite appearances, carefully orchestrated by himself, that he was making war on Marc Antony in pursuance of a 'national crusade', he was in fact at the battle of Actium inflicting a defeat on the one man who could realistically challenge him as a faction leader.

After the battle of Actium, Augustus' primacy rested partly on his undisputed factional leadership and partly on the near-universal recognition that he was at the time the only man of sufficient wealth and prestige (*auctoritas*) to be able to act as the centre of a stable government and prevent a return to civil strife. He ensured, therefore, that the government of the *respublica* depended upon him and the network of supporters who followed him. In other words, he was a faction leader, a leading citizen (*princeps*) to whom, because of the unusually dangerous and confused situation that existed following Caesar's murder in 44 BC, had been entrusted a special mandate to govern in order to save and restore the *respublica*.

Strictly, of course, such a role and position could not be passed on by way of inheritance; *auctoritas* could exist in a man only by a combination of birth, status and personal achievement, whilst the actual powers by which the *princeps* governed were in the gift of the senate, the *populus* and the *plebs*. The truth of this was in fact recognised by Augustus when he was said by Tacitus to have mentioned the names of a number of consular senators who might be considered adequate to continue his role. In AD 14, in any case, there was no precedent for the transmission of power; indeed, the formal transmission of it would call into question the whole façade of the 'restored republic'. It is little wonder, therefore, that at the time of Augustus' death in AD 14 Tiberius found himself on the horns of a dilemma – or, as he himself is said by Suetonius to have put it, 'holding a wolf by its ears'. Yet he appreciated too that government had to continue, and on certain significant issues he made immediate use of the proconsular and tribunician powers that had been properly bestowed upon him at Augustus' instigation.

Yet, to continue in his use of those powers, he needed a demonstration that he, like Augustus, was a man of *auctoritas*, so that if the special mandate was to continue he could be seen as the man to take it on. In addition, for a private and diffident man like Tiberius, who was already 56 years of age, there was a further question: whether he himself really wanted or was personally suited to a role which had, after all, been moulded by the circumstances, the position and the personality of Augustus Caesar. As Tiberius himself is said to have observed, 'only Augustus was capable of bearing this burden'; he was clearly aware that he could neither inherit nor match his adoptive father's *auctoritas*.

Further, the intrigues and uncertainties that had surrounded Augustus' dynastic policies only made matters more difficult for Tiberius. Many believed that Augustus had not wanted to adopt Tiberius and that it was only, as he himself stated in his will, the workings of a 'cruel fortune' that had prevented him handing his position on to others. It was felt too that it was only thanks to his mother that Tiberius had survived to be elevated to the principate. Tiberius was paying the price for the vicissitudes of

17

his years under Augustus and the generally low profile he had enjoyed during that time. In short, Tiberius in AD 14 needed to know that he was 'called by the republic' rather than stand accused of having crept into his position largely as a result of Livia's manipulative pressure on her increasingly senile husband.

Thus, if Tiberius was to take on Augustus' role, he needed to receive the kind of unequivocal acclamation that had greeted Augustus when, in 27 BC, he had seemed to be trying to lay his powers aside. That, after all, was the only precedent which he had to follow.

For Tiberius in AD 14, such an 'acclamation' was more crucial than it had been for Augustus in 27 BC, for not only had Tiberius not won the right to rule, but, unlike Augustus, he was perceived as having rivals to his position. These were not to be found amongst consular senators, one of whom at least acknowledged the superior *auctoritas* of Tiberius; rather, Tiberius' rivals were to be found within Augustus' family.

One of these was Agrippa Postumus, whom in AD 4 Augustus had adopted as his son along with Tiberius. As we have seen, Agrippa had been banished by Augustus in AD 7, although in Augustus' last years speculation had centred on the possible implications of a rumoured reconciliation.

Germanicus Caesar had also figured in the same adoption arrangements – as Tiberius' new son. Whilst Tiberius, following his stabilising of the critical situation in Germany in AD 9, had been brought back to Rome, Germanicus had been appointed by Augustus to the overall command of the eight Rhine legions. It was Tiberius' fear that this young man, who enjoyed a wide, if rather ill-founded, popularity, might prefer the reality to the expectation of power. It is Tacitus' contention that it was his fear of rivals that led Tiberius to make use of the powers which he held, and thus act in a manner inconsistent with his own professed wishes. For many, this was the proof that Tiberius Caesar was indeed the hypocrite that popular opinion alleged.

The days that followed the death of Augustus represented for Tiberius a series of public relations disasters. First, the news reached Rome of the murder of Agrippa Postumus; the chain of events which led to the murder remains unclear, although Tiberius protested his own innocence, offering other, but not very credible, alternatives. He even tried to force the officer who had conveyed the execution order to make a personal report to the senate. This attempt to implicate a subordinate in such a public way in the responsibility for his actions was seen as unwise, and Tiberius was given the memorable piece of advice by a senior member of his household staff that 'the accounts would balance only if they had a single auditor'. Whatever the truth, Tiberius' attempts to clear his own name were seen as damaging to the fabric of government.

Even the discussions on Augustus' funeral, which perhaps should not have been controversial, found Tiberius at odds with senators who, he thought, failed to respond to the situation with sufficient dignity. The demand of some of them to be permitted to carry the coffin of the dead *princeps* was brusquely set aside by Tiberius, who clearly felt that the memory of his predecessor deserved better than to become the catalyst of unseemly clamour. This was just one of many occasions when the obsessive nature of Tiberius' respect for Augustus' memory was to lead him into difficulties. For this reason too, Tiberius is unlikely to have been much impressed by some of the discussion of Augustus' life that took place at this time; whilst many gave Augustus' achievements a wide measure of praise, others saw more cynical motives for much that had been done over the previous half-century.

Worse was to follow after the funeral of Augustus, when discussions naturally turned to the future of the government. In fact, this stage of discussions was not as protracted as sometimes alleged; the idea that Tiberius continued cavilling in the senate into late September is due to a misunderstanding of Tacitus' references to Augustus' deification which took place on 17 September. It can in fact be shown that the discussions of the future were not prolonged beyond the first two or three days of September. None the less, the fact that the period was shorter than sometimes thought does nothing to limit the damage that Tiberius' stance during the discussions occasioned amongst senators.

The framework of the discussions appears to have been a motion in the names of the consuls that Tiberius should be granted the powers necessary for him to carry on the government – in other words, a confirmation of the powers that he had already been exercising over the previous decade under the umbrella of Augustus' *auctoritas*. As we have seen, an acclamation in his own right was of great significance to Tiberius and his own *auctoritas*, for only to have exercised such powers under the responsibility of Augustus was a very different matter.

The discussions in the senate were uncomfortable and ill-humoured. They were made the more difficult for Tiberius since, without doubt, there was in him at least some genuine reluctance to assume the burden at all and a very sharp feeling of his own inferiority when measured against the achievements of Augustus. For this reason, even when he did become emperor, he tried to discourage the application to himself of the name Augustus – to no effect, as the reign's inscriptions amply demonstrate.

Besides this, however, there was an element of falsehood in his performance, for he was trying in a very gauche way to bring about the kind of acclamation that would for him confirm others' confidence in his abilities. However, Tiberius always found it difficult to conceal his true feelings; Tacitus points out on a number of occasions that when Tiberius was speaking sincerely his words had an easy flow to them, but when he was covering up what he really felt in diplomatic falsehoods, then his words became more and more clumsy and awkward. He could not lie easily in the service of political expediency, and his audiences could always tell when he was attempting such concealment; they did not, however, wish to be seen to have detected it. So, many had recourse simply to flattery which Tiberius found both useless and distasteful. Others tried to argue on his own terms, suggesting alternatives to his assumption of sole power; they too found themselves in difficulties – in particular, Asinius Gallus, with whom, as we have seen, Tiberius had a long-standing personal antagonism, and who, Tiberius felt, was using the occasion to cause personal embarrassment. Others simply became exasperated at what they saw as a useless and embarrassing charade; 'let him take it or leave it', one is said to have shouted out. More damaging, however, was the observation that if Tiberius did not wish to take on the position, then all he had to do was to use his tribunician power, which he had already employed for other purposes, to veto the consuls' motion. This of course highlighted the falseness of Tiberius' position – or, as some would have it, his malicious hypocrisy. Many assumed that the purpose of this hypocritical show was to trap senators into indiscretions which could later be used against them.

In the end, therefore, the discussions achieved nothing beyond a decided sourness in the relations between Tiberius and the senate. He did not receive his acclamation, for, as Tacitus shows, Tiberius became emperor simply by tiring of these exchanges and letting the consular motion proceed. It no doubt made matters a good deal worse for Tiberius that his mother, Livia, received under the terms of Augustus' will the honorific name of Julia Augusta. As a traditionalist, Tiberius did not like the public display of women's influence in politics and will have been even more mortified by the suggestion that he should himself be styled 'son of Livia'; he felt his mother's domination keenly enough anyway.

Tiberius thus became *princeps*, but the 'accession discussions' had proved disastrous to his morale and to his relationship with the senatorial nobility, for whom he probably had a far greater respect than had Augustus. Relations between the new *princeps* and the senate, once soured in this way, did not improve.

Nor were Tiberius' early problems limited to his dealings with the senate. Although it has been shown that chronologically his attitude towards accepting Augustus' position could not have been affected by the mutinies which broke out amongst the legions on the Rhine and Danube, these did none the less pose a very serious problem for the new *princeps*. It would appear unlikely that the mutinies were initially connected or had anything intrinsically to do with Tiberius himself. Rather, they represented a reaction to the deteriorating service conditions in the wake of the problems in the two areas during Augustus' last decade. The two situations were probably made worse by the necessity for emergency recruitment into the legions of people who might otherwise have been considered undesirable. There is in any case no doubt that both armies contained trouble-makers, as well as those with genuine grievances at being retained under arms much longer than they should have been.

Both mutinies, however, rapidly took on political overtones – not least because the ringleaders realised that the change of *princeps* provided a situation favourable for the application of pressure. Tiberius also had difficulty in deciding how to handle the outbreaks: he was already anxious about Germanicus' intentions, and it did not enhance his confidence to hear that

21

some of the mutineers had offered to put themselves at Germanicus' disposal should he wish to make a bid for power. In fact, Germanicus' loyalty to Tiberius was not in question, although Tiberius was later made more anxious by Germanicus' decision to try to defuse the trouble by paying out of his own pocket Augustus' bequests to his troops: strictly – and Tiberius emphasised the point – only Augustus' successor had the right to distribute these.

Tiberius was further exercised by the problem of whether he should expose his own authority by a visit to the centres of trouble, and, if so, which he should attend first – for fear of giving offence to the other army. He avoided this dilemma – though he was severely criticised for it at home – by going to neither troublespot, but rather leaving Germanicus to handle the Rhine mutineers and sending his son Drusus, in the company of Lucius Aelius Sejanus, the prefect of the praetorian guard, to the Danube.

Both situations were potentially ugly, but Drusus was more fortunate in that the happy coincidence of an eclipse of the moon shocked the mutineers, who feared that the gods were angry at their disloyalty, back into obedience. Germanicus' problems, however, proved more severe and testing: as the situation deteriorated, he and his family came in danger of their lives, and finally he felt compelled to sanction a campaign on the east bank of the Rhine. Not only was this contrary to the instructions Augustus had on his death-bed laid upon Tiberius – that of keeping the Empire within its present frontiers – but it also took Germanicus and his legions back into the territory where only five years previously Varus and his three legions had been totally annihilated in one of the worst disasters ever inflicted upon a Roman army.

On this occasion, the tactic worked, and Germanicus brought his army back in better order and unscathed. Tiberius, however, no doubt armed with his own military experience, worried – rightly as events were to show – that cheap success in this instance might convince Germanicus that earlier dreams of an Elbe frontier could be revived. Tiberius was not prepared to sanction this, and the issue was to cause friction between the *princeps* and his heir.

The formal close of these mutinous episodes was a report by Tiberius to the senate. Although he attempted to deal evenhandedly with Germanicus' and Drusus' actions, the fact remained that Drusus had not compromised his position by major concessions to the troops whereas Germanicus had. The *princeps*, no matter how hard he might try, could not praise both with equal conviction: his attempts to be diplomatic in Germanicus' case were vitiated by his customary inability to tell half-truths convincingly.

As on earlier occasions at the time of the accession, Tiberius' awkwardness was obvious, and it was put down to hypocrisy. This impression was to have a significant bearing on the future course of relations between Tiberius and Germanicus, and – even more importantly – on people's interpretation of that relationship.

In all, therefore, the events of the early weeks and months of Tiberius' principate created impressions that would prove impossible to change, and were to cast an indelible shadow over the rest of the reign both for the *princeps* himself and for his subjects.

4

Tiberius, the senate and the nobility

The key to Augustus' success had been his ability to work with and find meaningful roles for the senate as a body and for the nobles as individuals. Although, ultimately, law-making remained the business of the assemblies of the *populus* and the *plebs*, the senate's role as the body by which laws were formulated and discussed became regular; both the *princeps* himself and the consuls were responsible for passing a great deal of legislation through the senate, with popular participation becoming increasingly a formality. Under Augustus, the senate had already acquired completely new judicial functions, which it had taken over from the people.

A significant feature in the Augustan settlement was the manner in which the *princeps* managed to reconcile the noble families to the notion of his primacy in government; his prestige and consequent patronage not only bound large numbers of the nobility to him, but also enabled him to retain the old 'promotions system' (*cursus honorum*) as part of the machinery by which the restored republic was administered. Thus, the nobility could compete for his patronage and, as before, climb the ladder of a senatorial career, aiming ultimately at the consulship and the great army commands reserved for ex-consuls and effectively in the gift of the *princeps*.

Augustus' success was due in part to the strength of his *auctoritas* and in part also to the overwhelming desire for 'peace with honour' which followed the upheavals which culminated in the battle of Actium. The unique power of his position enabled him to bring new families into the senate under his patronage and support their promotion to consular status, and to offer the older, noble, families a convincing means of keeping their historic prestige alive.

In the last years of Augustus' reign there appear to have been two substantial factional groupings of senators. One of these consisted mostly, but by no means entirely, of newer senatorial families and looked directly to Augustus as their faction leader. This 'Julian' faction was in some ways the descendant of the *populares* of the republic. The other faction contained more of the older families and seems increasingly to have looked to Tiberius as its figurehead, presumably believing that his inclinations and antecedents gave him a greater proximity to families whose roots were deeply embedded in Rome's traditions. This 'Claudian' group was the successor to the *optimates* of the republic. These were not, however, political parties in a modern sense with programmes for the electorate to choose; rather, they were groupings within which senators sought to fulfil their ambitions and reach the consulship. Tacitus' account of senatorial business during Tiberius' reign indicates that individual senators still strove with each other for superiority. Moreover, some sign of factional groupings of senators emerges in accounts of major trials in the senate where it is possible to see particular senators rallying to the support of friends and factional colleagues in trouble.

Tiberius certainly had particular senatorial friends and supporters, most of whom were men of older families, like Marcus Lepidus and Cnaeus Piso, with whom the *princeps* had been on good terms since his early days. However, the history of Tiberius' relationship with the senate has more to do with his views on the roles of senate and senators, and how viable these were.

We have already seen that Tiberius' encounters with the senate at the opening of his reign were disastrous for their relationship; a spirit of fear, suspicion and hostility was thus early implanted in their dealings. Yet Tiberius seems genuinely to have desired to see a senate which could take the role of an independently-minded and honest partner in the business of government. His chief desire, as he himself said, was to enjoy a good reputation with his peers. In deprecating the excessiveness which he saw in the practice of erecting temples to emperors and treating them as gods, Tiberius eloquently stated that a good reputation would, for him, constitute a temple in the hearts of those who admired him.

Tiberius may not have worked out a senatorial role in any detail, but his view of the senate and the magistrates was rooted in the republican past. He made way for the consuls in the street; he deprecated references to himself as 'Master' and said that he thought of the senators as his masters. He detested the sycophancy of some members, remarking on more than one occasion that they were 'men fit to be slaves'. He was irritated when they referred to him matters which he felt to be within their own competence. All of this confirms Tacitus' judgement that the first half of the reign was marked by sound administration in which Tiberius strove to maintain the integrity of the senate and the magistrates. Tiberius clearly believed himself to be a traditional *princeps* – the senate's most prestigious member, able to sway by virtue of his seniority and prestige but not dominating by his powers. Indeed, the situation sharply recalls that enunciated by Augustus, that he 'excelled all by virtue of his prestige, but of actual powers he possessed no more than his colleagues in the magistracies'.

His attitude to individual senators was similar to this; he detested any behaviour that stressed an overwhelming superiority on his part – such as the practice of self-prostration in his presence. He showed a righteous anger at those senators who attempted to gain wealth or influence by undermining their colleagues in the senate. He tried to ensure that in a traditional fashion the senator could better himself on the basis of his merits and connections. In the case of elections for both praetorships and consulships, he did his best – as he saw it – to prevent his own wishes becoming dominant in the procedure. Indeed, that he succeeded at least in part is shown by the fact that one of the senate's reactions, when Tiberius transferred elections from the people to the senate in AD 15, was that it would not have to expend so much money to secure the election of the candidates it favoured.

Thus, the conduct of the *princeps* at least during the first half of his reign appears to have been directed towards securing a co-operation in government with the senate which was based on his traditional respect for them and on their fair-minded independence of spirit. It is clear, however, from a study of the accounts of Tiberius' reign that such genuine co-operation was a rarity – even during Tiberius' first decade as *princeps*. Why did Tiberius' good intentions come to so little in practice?

It is clear that a number of factors contributed. Not least among these was the reputation with which Tiberius succeeded Augustus; he was held to be arrogant, secretive and a hypocrite who had become emperor against the better judgement of Augustus. A personal *auctoritas*, which was essential to Tiberius' successful relationship with the nobility, was undermined before Tiberius even started. Further, we have seen that much residual goodwill was damaged beyond repair in the bizarre and embarrassing fiasco that constituted the 'accession debate'. What, however, was even more damaging was that whilst Tiberius succeeded Augustus with many good intentions, it is clear that much of what he did was ill-thought-out. He had not taken proper account of the nature of the senate and the nobility after half a century of Augustus' domination; it obviously, for example, did not occur to him that his acceptance and use of the censorial powers reluctantly employed by Augustus gave him a dominance over the senate which no amount of moderate behaviour could ameliorate. Nor did Tiberius make any allowance at all for the effects of his own views and prejudices.

Tacitus' account of Tiberius' early years as *princeps* provides ample evidence of what might be called a failure by default on Tiberius' part. For example, Tiberius' contribution to the 'accession debate' was flawed by his own failure to be honest and straightforward and by his lack of understanding of how far the senate had grown used to domination; it had in effect forgotten how to initiate.

As Tacitus shows, Tiberius' domination of the senate was not deliberate or malicious but unintended and arbitrary. In practice, the senate found this harder to handle, because it was inconsistent. Indeed, Tacitus brings together in his account of the events of AD 15 a number of senatorial discussions which illustrate the growth of a 'credibility gap' between *princeps* and senate.

Included in this are two instances of individuals who were accused of disrespect to the memory of Augustus. In one case, Tiberius was contemptuously dismissive of the charges, announcing that 'injuries done to gods are for gods to avenge' and that 'Augustus had not been decreed a place in heaven so that this could be used to ruin his former fellow citizens'. In this, Tiberius acted in a clear-headed and fair-minded way. But shortly afterwards a similar charge found the *princeps* so incensed against the accused that he tried to stampede the senate into voting for his condemnation. It took a very strong-minded senator and friend of the *princeps*, Cnaeus Piso, to point out the impossibility of the position in which the senate was thus placed.

Similarly ill-judged was Tiberius' plan to 'sit in' on the praetor's court; he took trouble to occupy an unobtrusive position on the platform, and, according to Tacitus, induced some good verdicts by his presence. The larger issue – the integrity and independence of the praetor's chairmanship of the court – seems not to have occurred to the *princeps*.

Just as Tiberius' prejudices had come to the fore in the second of the cases involving an insult to the dead Augustus, so too they vitiated a senatorial debate on the subject of theatrical rowdyism. The discussion flowed back and forth in apparent freedom until at a late stage Tiberius intervened to announce the outcome which he required. This was based on Augustus' views on the subject, which, he said, he could not disregard; the senate was left with the feeling that it had been cheated by a sham debate and that its apparent freedom to debate such matters was completely illusory.

It is hardly surprising, therefore, that the senate should have shrunk from involving itself openly in matters where the *princeps* might have an interest. This is well illustrated in the context of a discussion in AD 22 over the question of the appointment of a proconsul of Africa – a province within the senate's remit. Partly because a war in the province had necessitated the dispatch to Africa of a legion from an imperial province and partly because one of the contenders for the post was an uncle of Tiberius' favourite, Sejanus, the senate asked Tiberius to make an appointment. Angrily he referred it back to them, completely unable to understand the senate's difficulty. Yet we can also find instances in which, by accident or design, Tiberius did apparently come to exercise greater power over the senate and its members. For example, in the election of magistrates, although Tiberius evidently tried to leave some room for freedom of choice, the practices which he adopted were designed to secure the election of the candidates he wanted. What is more, particularly with the consular elections, the procedures which he initiated were so tortuous and secretive that, whatever his intention may have been, he heightened the impression of arbitrariness and domination and, according to Tacitus, eroded the senate's freedom. Further, Tiberius attempted to interfere with the *cursus honorum* – albeit in the interests of efficiency – by making appointments in blocks of five years and by making promotions out of turn.

Encroachments on the senate's freedom, therefore, did occur; and although these were not with the aim of imposing a dictatorial government, the effect was to leave the senate understandably feeling that its activities were subject to an intervention which seemed the more tyrannical because it was arbitrary. The growing sense of powerlessness which resulted from this made senators more servile and less inclined to respond positively to Tiberius; for his part, Tiberius failed to grasp how far it was his behaviour that was the cause of poor relations. The developing gulf between *princeps* and senate was one of the reasons why, after AD 23, Tiberius began to leave more of the day-to-day administration to his friend, Sejanus, and eventually entrusted it to him entirely when in AD 26 he decided to retire from Rome.

Such episodes as these contributed to the gradual souring of relations between Tiberius and the nobility. However, the feature of the reign which most obviously demonstrated the dominance of the *princeps* and the precariousness of the positions of senators was the operation of the law of treason (*Lex Julia de maiestate*).

Of course, the existence and use of a treason law were not features unique to the principate; a law had existed in the later republic which comprehended actions which 'diminished the majesty of the Roman senate and people' (*maiestas minuta*). Augustus had revised the law in his *Lex Julia* and had also been responsible for its development; the law, the application of which had originally been restricted to actions, was under Augustus expanded to include treasonable words, written or spoken. Also, although the law could be used to deal with actions against any part of the state's interests, it tended increasingly to be restricted in its application to actions or words which were alleged to have damaged the *princeps* or his family.

There is certainly no evidence to suggest that, in his early years at least, Tiberius used this law as a means of protecting himself. Indeed, it can be shown that he was frequently dismissive of charges that concerned himself. The problems arose partly out of the uncomfortable nature of the relationship between Tiberius and the senate, which we have already described, and partly out of the way in which the law operated. So serious was this combination of features that Tacitus singled out the operation of this law and the fear that Tiberius' behaviour during cases often inspired as the most damaging developments in the early part of Tiberius' reign.

Cases were heard in either of two courts. There was a permanent court (*quaestio de maiestate*) over which a praetor presided; in addition, since Augustus' time the senate had enjoyed a judicial function, and could hear serious cases brought against its own members. According to Tacitus, Tiberius created a bad impression early in his reign by giving permission for treason cases to be heard; he could, like some of his successors, have put the operation of the law 'on ice', and many took his decision not to do this as evidence of his tyrannical purpose. Further, he believed that the courts could reach impartial verdicts and that intervention on his part was inappropriate. In principle, this was reasonable, except that, as we have seen, in this matter as in others, senators were bound to try to accommodate the wishes of the *princeps*; if he chose not to state his views, then senators were left to do what they imagined he wanted – a sensitive matter in cases which concerned allegations of actions or words directed against him. We should not forget that his presence in the senate as a member was bound to have an intimidating effect, especially if, as so often, he sat silent. A similar effect will have been created in the permanent court by his decision to 'sit in' on its sessions. Tiberius, however, characteristically was completely oblivious to this, regarding his behaviour as liberal and fair-minded.

The other damaging effect of the operation of this law was caused by the nature of prosecution procedures in Rome. There was no official prosecution service, and prosecutions were initiated by private individuals (*delatores*) who put information before the relevant authorities. Such information led to an accusation and trial. However, two factors made this a damaging system. First, the reward for information laying was measured in terms of a proportion of the property of a convicted person; it was thus worthwhile to initiate the prosecution of rich and influential citizens. Second, many of the informers understood the fears and suspicions of Tiberius and played upon them by bringing to him reports of men who were allegedly conspiring against, or who had made uncomplimentary remarks about, the *princeps*. Emotionally, if not always institutionally, he became involved. Tacitus and others regarded the informers as a cancer in society, and thought that, although Tiberius did on occasion encourage action against over-zealous informers, in the main his inaction encouraged them. Tiberius indeed did seem blind to the dangers when, in a particularly unsavoury instance, he refused to deal with the informers and remarked that it would be 'better to revoke the laws than remove their guardians'. Undoubtedly, Tiberius had to bear some responsibility for the 'reign of terror' to which these activities eventually led.

Tiberius certainly did not regard his behaviour as culpable; indeed he probably saw himself as vigilant in the checking of abuse without realising that the very need for such a role was symptomatic of a serious problem. It is undeniable that the *princeps* did check what he regarded at the time as abuse, but he did so in a way which was thought to be highly arbitrary.

Ironically, Tiberius' general principle was one of non-interference once the process of justice had started: he argued that he could not intervene if information on charges had already been laid and that he could not try to influence the senate's deliberation of a case, since, as we have seen, he liked to think that there was nothing to inhibit the proper process of justice. Indeed, on occasion he adhered so rigidly to this that even the ten-day moratorium between sentence and execution, which was intended as a 'cooling-off' period, proved ineffective because the senate remained under the pressures which had led it to its original decision and Tiberius did not see fit to say what he thought whilst the process of justice was still in motion.

Despite the appearance of a non-interventionist policy, the reality was often otherwise; Tiberius did in fact intervene frequently, and although this was usually done with respectable motives, the effect was arbitrary and tyrannical. Sometimes, the

31

princeps intervened to quash cases if he thought a prosecution trivial or malicious, though little consistency appears to have been attached to these interventions. For example, we have already seen the inconsistency evident in his treatment of cases concerning alleged insults to the memory of Divus Augustus. In cases concerning allegations of slander or libel against himself or members of his family, he generally intervened to obtain the dropping of charges concerning himself, though allowing members of his family to reach their own decisions. On one occasion, however, he became so angry as the evidence was recited that he demanded the chance to clear his name, thus virtually turning the case into a trial of himself. Tacitus reports that after this experience Tiberius determined to attend the senate less, and the experience probably played a part in Tiberius' eventual decision to retire from Rome altogether.

Such arbitrariness could not but damage relations between the *princeps* and the senate; for the senate was anxious to do what the *princeps* wished but often lacked any clear notion of what that was. Further, cases such as these, where the charges concerned allegations of insults made against the *princeps*, inevitably worked to elevate Tiberius on to a pedestal above his fellow senators, making them the more anxious to act as he wished and giving him less chance of achieving the 'equal co-operation' between himself and the senate which was plainly his objective.

We have seen that Tiberius did not like to intervene during the process of a case, though it should be said that a number of innocent defendants, including Tiberius' friend Cnaeus Piso, earnestly wished that Tiberius would break through his self-imposed impartiality when he saw the threat of gross miscarriage of justice. The lack of realism in Tiberius' conduct is highlighted by the interventions which he made after the completion of cases in order to pardon defendants. It is a matter of record that Tiberius liked to appear as the saviour of defendants and that he complained that those who (in desperation) committed suicide during their trials robbed him of the chance to bring deliverance. This was less cynical in intention than it sounds, though understandably the impression it created did little for the image of the *princeps*. The true irony of Tiberius' position is that had he not been so obstinately impartial when it really mattered, he could have exercised his clemency to far better effect. It was no doubt partly to counter bad publicity on this matter and partly to record Tiberius' genuine beliefs about his stance that in AD 22 he caused two coin-issues to be struck which commemorated his clemency (CLEMENTIA) and his moderation (MODERATIO).

In short, Tiberius' relations with the senate were blighted by the operation of the treason law. At best his behaviour could be seen as generally well-intentioned but short-sighted and damaging in its effects; at worst his actions could be interpreted as part of a cynical and sinister plot to achieve the ruin of rich and influential senators – the kind of men who could, it might be thought, pose a danger to him. This only served to confirm the interpretation that many already had applied to his general approach to his relationship with the senate. Again, a lack of realism had led him into appearing to expect an unrealistic degree of senatorial independence which many of his own actions served to undermine.

Ironically, many senior senators were prepared to recognise him as a man of *auctoritas*; his striving to achieve it, however, made many lose faith in his capabilities and in his sincerity. The crisis of confidence that ensued played a major part in creating the sense of frozen powerlessness amongst senators, the effects of which were to be so often deplored by Tiberius. This failure in his relationship was a contributory cause of Tiberius' decision to retire from Rome and active politics – a decision which, as we shall see later, ushered in a far more thorough-going tyranny when Tiberius was no longer on the spot to cajole the senate and check abuses of individual and corporate freedom. Contrary, however, to the belief of many, it was Tiberius' blindness and obstinacy, and no tyrannical intentions, that caused this to happen.

5

Tiberius and the family of Germanicus

Throughout the principate of Tiberius, an atmosphere of suspicion and conflict blighted relations between the *princeps* and his nephew, Germanicus, and his family. The long-term significance of this lay in the fact that public interpretation of the relationship led to deep suspicion of Tiberius' intentions and consequently increased unpopularity for the *princeps*. Besides this, the disunity within Tiberius' family contributed greatly to the isolation of the *princeps* and thus provided an opportunity for Sejanus, the prefect of the praetorian guard, to insinuate himself into Tiberius' favour – with disastrous results (see Chapter 6).

Germanicus was born in approximately 15 BC, the son of Tiberius' brother, Nero Drusus, and Marc Antony's daughter, Antonia; we do not know his full name, as references to him consistently employ the honorific name (Germanicus), which he inherited from his father. Nero Drusus and Antonia appear to have enjoyed a widespread popularity, which was based partly on their affability, partly on the affection for them supposedly shown by Augustus, and partly on the prevailing belief that Nero Drusus disliked the 'monarchy' and desired a return to the ways of the old republic. There was little evidence for this, though the story was sufficiently durable for Germanicus' reputation to benefit from his father's supposed 'republicanism'. Two other children of the family survived to adulthood – the

34

future emperor, Claudius, and Livilla, who married Tiberius' son, Drusus, but was later accused of murdering him in complicity with Sejanus.

Although Germanicus was around 30 years of age when Tiberius succeeded Augustus, the *princeps* probably did not know his nephew well, as their circumstances had kept them apart for much of Germanicus' life. Evidently Augustus entertained high hopes for Germanicus and was presumably responsible for his marriage to Julia's daughter, Agrippina, who was always to show a powerful enthusiasm for the fortunes of the Julian family, comparable to that which Livia entertained for the Claudians.

Augustus' favour was again made obvious in the adoption arrangements undertaken in AD 4 (see Chapter 2, pp. 12 and 13). Rumour held that, had Germanicus been older in AD 4, he would have been Augustus' own preferred heir. There may have been truth in this, although Augustus was sufficiently realistic to know that such a course of action would not have been acceptable to many of the nobility. One member of this group, Cnaeus Calpurnius Piso, is said to have acknowledged the superior *auctoritas* of Tiberius but to have been quite unimpressed by the standing of the next generation of the imperial family – that is, Germanicus and Drusus. The fact that Augustus forced Tiberius to recognise Germanicus as his heir caused resentment in Tiberius and helped further to polarise the imperial family into the two 'camps' – Claudians and Julians.

Even after the formalisation of the adoption arrangements, Tiberius had little opportunity of working with and getting to know his 'new son'. Tiberius himself was away, first in Pannonia and then in Germany between AD 5 and 10, whilst Germanicus himself took up his command of the Rhine legions shortly after this. Such was the effect of Augustus' favour towards Germanicus and Tiberius' diffidence about his own standing that at the time of Augustus' death in AD 14 Tiberius was afraid that Germanicus might use the base of support which his legions comprised and attempt to win power. The fact that Germanicus remained loyal to his adoptive father did little to assuage Tiberius' anxieties: indeed, the suspicions of the *princeps* were exacerbated by his fears of the ulterior motives of Agrippina.

The mutiny amongst the Rhine legions that followed Augustus' death put Germanicus' abilities severely to the test. There is no doubt that the situation was extremely dangerous and required a more experienced hand than Germanicus' to settle it. In Tiberius' eyes, the popularity amongst the legions enjoyed by Germanicus and his family was a further cause for anxiety; however, whilst Germanicus' judgement could certainly be called into question, his loyalty could not. At a number of points in the episode Germanicus showed his lack of experience, and in all of these his actions gave Tiberius reason for worry.

First, Germanicus showed the histrionic side to his character when he threatened to kill himself if the mutineers did not return to obedience. This characteristically extravagant gesture nearly ended in disaster. Second, the granting of financial concessions to the mutineers was an act which strictly was beyond Germanicus' competence – a point certainly not lost on the *princeps*. Third, the exposing of his family to danger was ill-considered and again will have worried Tiberius on account of the high profile being afforded to Agrippina and her children. Fourth, the decision to allow the mutineers to work off their anger on each other was in the event recognised by Germanicus himself as little short of a catastrophe. His final 'solution', that of taking the legions across the Rhine to absorb their energies in a worthwhile project, was contrary to the advice Augustus had given Tiberius about frontier stability, and thus worried the *princeps* on account of its possible motives and certainly on account of the risks it incurred. Even so, Tiberius made none of these criticisms or anxieties public, though, as often in such circumstances, he was unable to conceal them. Instead, presumably to avoid confrontation with his adopted son, he reluctantly allowed the campaigning across the Rhine to continue. In the event, Tiberius' misgivings were completely vindicated; despite Germanicus' obvious conviction that success could be won at no great cost, little was achieved, and losses were incurred both at the hands of the enemy and as a result of atrocious weather conditions. Further, conditions were so unpredictable that one of Germanicus' battle-groups very nearly suffered the same fate as that of Varus six years previously – and at the hands of the same enemy, Arminius, chief of the Cherusci tribe. Indeed, Germanicus himself encountered the grisly remains of Varus' shattered army and the emotion generated by this in Germanicus and amongst his troops again gave Tiberius reason for gravely doubting Germanicus' judgement.

Germanicus emerged from the whole episode as loyal and honourable but also as unsuited to such a post, due to lack of experience and his rather histrionic turn of character. Such a description explains both his widespread popularity as a like-able, even gallant, young man, and Tiberius' misgivings about him. In view of the fact that Tiberius did not make public any of his misgivings, people not only contrasted his grim and serious personality unfavourably with that of Germanicus, but also suspected that behind imperial reticence lay sinister intent. Public opinion, therefore, was serving to enhance the confrontational elements that were clearly present in this relationship.

In AD 16, Tiberius decided to call a halt to the German campaigning which he had never wanted: an opportunity was provided by the seriously disturbed state of affairs in the east, where the occupancy of the throne of Armenia had once again become a bone of contention between Rome and the King of Parthia. Following Augustan precedent in sending significant figures such as Marcus Agrippa and Gaius Caesar to this troublespot, Tiberius decided to invest his adopted son with a special commission to settle a series of eastern problems. The *princeps* was, however, faced with two difficulties: first, he had to remove Germanicus from the Rhine without causing major affront to him, his family and supporters; second, he had to provide Germanicus with advisers in the east who would rein in his enthusiasms as well as keep an eye on his and Agrippina's propriety and loyalty. In both of these difficulties, Tiberius himself made disastrous miscalculations. Not that the whole responsibility for the ensuing chain of events should be put at the door of Tiberius: Germanicus, for example, refused to heed Tiberius' advice that events had shown German campaigning to be costly in effort and manpower and low in results. The *princeps* had in the end to instruct his adopted son to return home, and, in what can only be described as a serious diplomatic blunder, he added for good measure that if campaigning had to continue Germanicus should allow Drusus (Tiberius' son) to have an opportunity to prove himself. This self-evident inconsistency in Tiberius' arguments convinced Germanicus and others that the motives of the *princeps* were sinister, even malicious.

Again Tiberius' choice as 'adviser' to Germanicus in the east was his old friend, the experienced, outspoken and independently minded Cnaeus Calpurnius Piso, whom he appointed governor of the major imperial province of Syria. Tiberius knew him to be both trustworthy and unlikely to be overawed by Germanicus' rank. Piso was accompanied in his appointment by his wife, Plancina, who was a close friend of Livia and presumably seen as an ideal foil to Agrippina.

It is reasonable to argue that, in the event, Piso's conduct represented a caricature of his mission; he pounced upon each and every indiscretion into which Germanicus' histrionic personality led him and was overbearing in his oversight of Germanicus' contacts with the army. Such behaviour might have been controlled by Tiberius had not the whole mission suddenly erupted completely out of control.

Germanicus and his family decided to take a break from duty with a sight-seeing trip to Egypt. Although this sounds innocent enough, Germanicus completely overlooked the special status of Egypt as the private property of the *princeps* which nobody could enter without specific permission. Tiberius criticised Germanicus for this, and for the informality of his behaviour there. Documentary evidence survives in the form of papyrus fragments which show that Germanicus was totally oblivious of protocol; not only did he refer wrongly to Egypt as a province within his competence but he gave practical effect to this by issuing edicts. He even, in an impromptu speech at Alexandria, rather unwisely compared himself to Alexander the Great.

Piso, meanwhile, had taken advantage of Germanicus' absence to cancel all the provincial arrangements he had made. Germanicus retaliated by ordering Piso out of Syria, though it must remain doubtful whether his *imperium* in the area allowed him to override Tiberius' appointments in his own provinces. Amidst this tension, Germanicus fell ill and died at Antioch. There is little doubt that his death was due to his illness, although there were many, principally Germanicus' family and staff, who believed that it was due to poison administered at Piso's instigation, and further that Piso was acting on the instructions of Tiberius and Livia. Such suspicions magnified to near-hysteria in Rome, where few believed that Germanicus had died a natural death and many suspected that Tiberius feared and hated Germanicus enough to cause his removal. The extravagant and ill-judged outburst of celebration by Piso and Plancina served only to fan the flames of indignation.

Emotion and confusion governed the aftermath: Germanicus' staff illegally appointed a new governor of Syria, but Piso made the crucial error of incurring Tiberius' anger by trying to regain the imperial province by force. Public opinion demanded a scapegoat, and the trial of Piso for Germanicus' murder duly provided one. For most, the only relevant question requiring clarification was how far Tiberius' hand in the episode would be revealed. Tiberius did not alleviate the suspicion by his own studied impartiality at the trial, though he was no doubt correct in his conviction that the only proper questions to be considered concerned Piso's aggravatory behaviour to Germanicus and his use of force to try to regain Syria. Suspicion was compounded by the refusal of the *princeps* to release relevant documents pertaining to Piso's appointment. Piso, disheartened by the obduracy of the *princeps* and even more by Livia's protection of Plancina, committed suicide before his trial was over. Whilst ancient accounts indicate that the evidence against Piso on the murder charge was extremely flimsy, the course and outcome of the trial served only to confirm people's suspicion that it was the dark, malicious hand of Tiberius which had removed the great hope for the future – Germanicus Caesar.

Such rumours were powerful in their depressive effect both upon Tiberius and, not surprisingly, upon his public standing. Further, the conviction that foul play had occurred provided Germanicus' widow, Agrippina, with a cause – the avenging of her husband's death and the restoration of the status of Augustus' descendants. The implacable hatred which she thereafter entertained for Tiberius contributed greatly in his advancing years to his growing sense of isolation and his ill-starred dependence on Sejanus. In the event, this proved as disastrous for Agrippina and her family as it was for Tiberius and his.

At this time, whilst Germanicus' death represented a political trauma, it was not necessarily a disaster in terms of the continuity of the dynasty. Tiberius himself, of course, had a son, Drusus, who was married to Germanicus' sister, Livilla; they had twin sons, born probably in AD 20, of whom one, Tiberius Gemellus, survived beyond childhood. Germanicus and Agrippina had six surviving children – Nero, Drusus and Gaius (Caligula), Agrippina, Livia and Drusilla.

On the face of things, it was to his own son, Drusus, that Tiberius turned in the aftermath of the death of his heir; in

AD 22 he conferred the tribunician power upon Drusus and gave his son a guardianship over Germanicus' two older sons. Whilst this might suggest that Drusus was now the *de facto* heir, it should be remembered that twenty-five years earlier Tiberius himself had received an apparent promotion – but only to allow him to act as a guardian of Gaius and Lucius Caesar. In the event, such speculation became meaningless, because in AD 23 Drusus died; there is little reason to doubt the story which was later told by Sejanus' estranged wife, Apicata, that Drusus had in fact been murdered by Livilla and Sejanus. It would appear, therefore, that Sejanus at least expected Drusus to succeed his father.

However, to show respect for Augustus' wishes was characteristic of Tiberius, and he may have intended to honour the spirit of Augustus' dynastic policy – that in the wake of Germanicus' death the expectation of power should pass to his sons, Nero and Drusus. Certainly, following his son's death, Tiberius made his intentions clear by formally entrusting Nero and Drusus into the care of the senate. This apparently careful guardianship of the interests of Germanicus' sons might have offered some stability for the future. That it did not was largely due to the bitterly vengeful stance of Germanicus' widow, supported by friends in the senate. Whilst Tiberius and Agrippina were trading insults and suspicions, Sejanus was able to utilise the mutual hostility and launch a plan for his own self-advancement which came close to destroying both the *Julii* and the *Claudii*; ultimately, this was the legacy of the unhappy relationship between Tiberius and his heir, Germanicus Caesar.

6
Sejanus

When Augustus died in AD 14, the praetorian guard was commanded by two men of equestrian status, Lucius Seius Strabo and his son, Lucius Aelius Sejanus. The guard made up most of the troops actually stationed in Italy, as Augustus had decided that the permanent garrison posts for the legions and auxiliary contingents should be in the provinces. The purpose of this had been partly, of course, to guarantee peace in the provinces but partly also to avoid the impression of military dictatorship which the presence of large numbers of troops in Italy would have given. The praetorian guard, which in republican times had been the bodyguard given to holders of *imperium*, was assigned to Augustus and arranged into nine cohorts of 1,000 men each. The troops were billeted in the small towns around Rome, presumably to keep their profile low. Further, to avoid the potential danger to himself posed by such troops, Augustus ensured that there would be two commanders (prefects) and that these would be of equestrian, rather than senatorial, status.

In AD 15, however, Seius Strabo was appointed by Tiberius to the most prestigious post open to equestrians – the prefecture of Egypt; his son, Sejanus, was thus left in sole command of the praetorian guard. Although he was of equestrian rank, Sejanus had impressive senatorial connections (see Figure 3); through his father he was related to the consular Terentii and through his mother, Cosconia Gallitta, with the Lentuli and with Q. Junius Blaesus, who at the time of Tiberius' accession was governor of the imperial province of Pannonia and its legions. Such connections were strengthened by the fact that Sejanus' adoption by Quintus Aelius Tubero gave him adopted brothers of consular status. This will clearly have enhanced Sejanus' career aspirations.

In Tacitus' account of Tiberius' reign in his *Annals*, Sejanus appears to 'explode' on to the political scene in AD 23. This impression is, however, misleading; his seniority of rank will have brought him close to the counsels of the *princeps* long before this. We know, for example, that he accompanied Tiberius' son, Drusus, in AD 14 on his mission to put down the mutiny amongst the Pannonian legions. He is shown shortly afterwards as sufficiently close to the *princeps* to be able to warn him of the influence of Agrippina over the Rhine legions, and he was considered to be of sufficient importance to be 'chosen' as the prospective father-in-law of a son of the future emperor, Claudius. Tiberius valued Sejanus, as he himself said, as the 'partner' of his labours.

How then was Sejanus able to make so strong an impression upon Tiberius? The answer to this lay partly in the difficulties which Tiberius experienced in his relations with others – for example, his family and the senate. We have also to remember that Tiberius was not a young man when he came to power, and was in his late sixties by the middle of his reign; because of this, many of his friends and contemporaries were dying, leaving Tiberius increasingly in isolation. All of these factors left an emperor who was not readily trusting increasingly reliant upon a man in whom he did feel confidence. On the positive side, it is clear from sources that, outwardly, Sejanus' character earned him the trust of the *princeps*, for he appeared loyal and hard-working, yet did not descend to the sycophancy which, in Tiberius' eyes, disfigured the behaviour of many others. In other words, Sejanus came across to Tiberius as a man who was both efficient and independent of mind.

The precise nature of the prefect's ambitions has been a matter of considerable debate, though broadly it would appear to have been his aim to isolate Tiberius, to undermine those who might have helped him, and increasingly to dominate an emperor who was less capable of handling the tasks of

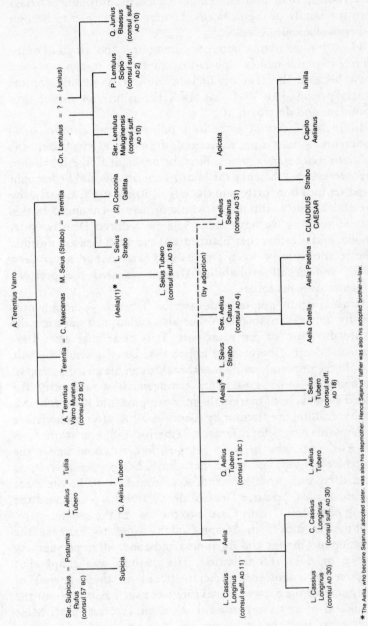

3 The family of Lucius Aelius Sejanus

* The Aelia, who became Sejanus' adopted sister, was also his stepmother. Hence Sejanus' father was also his adopted brother-in-law.

government than himself. Finally, perhaps, through marriage into the family of the *princeps*, he may have hoped to become Tiberius' logical successor.

However, the nature both of contemporary politics and of the source material makes a precise account hard to achieve – not least because the text of Tacitus' *Annals* is missing for the crucial period in AD 30–1 that saw Tiberius turn on his one-time confidant and destroy him.

In Tacitus' account – the only one with true chronological coherence – two significant and dramatic events mark the escalation of Sejanus' plans. First, he persuaded Tiberius that in the interests of efficiency the guards' cohorts should be brought together into one fortress in the city of Rome itself. Clearly, the prefect's ability to intimidate would be greatly enhanced by this act. Second, as we have seen, Sejanus seduced Drusus' wife, Livilla, and together they planned and executed Drusus' murder. The relationship between Drusus and Sejanus had never been good, and in all probability Drusus resented the prefect's influence over his father.

Drusus' death not only devastated Tiberius – though outwardly he took it stoically – but also called into question the future direction of the principate. It is clear that after Germanicus' death Tiberius had hoped that Drusus would be able to hold the imperial family together through his guardianship of Germanicus' older sons. This arrangement would carry the added advantage of marginalising Agrippina and her circle. No doubt recalling the attempt by Asinius Gallus, after his marriage to Vipsania, to adopt Drusus, Tiberius did not want Germanicus' sons, the heirs to his position, to come under the control of Agrippina and a new husband, particularly if, as seemed possible, that husband was, ironically, to be the same Asinius Gallus. So after Drusus' death Tiberius committed the young Nero and Drusus Caesar to the care of the senate.

The next moves in Sejanus' plans were to increase the isolation of Tiberius and Agrippina and above all to prevent any chance of their reconciliation. His method was simple but effective; he engineered judicial attacks on those friends of Agrippina whose views or activities were such as to prevent the likelihood of any sympathy for them on Tiberius' part. Most spectacular was the attack in AD 24 on a respected senator, Gaius Silius, and his wife, Sosia Galla. Both were long-standing associates of Germanicus and Agrippina from their time together on the Rhine earlier in the reign.

Significantly, Sejanus excused his attack to Tiberius on the grounds that some senators had shown too ready an enthusiasm for Agrippina's sons and that what he called 'Agrippina's party' should be cut down to size before it embroiled the state in civil war. Silius was vulnerable to a 'smear campaign' alleging sympathy with the leaders of a Gallic revolt three years previously, and he forfeited Tiberius' sympathy particularly because of his and his wife's rapacious and high-handed actions in Gaul. Sejanus chose his prosecutor well; Visellius Varro, consul of AD 24, was the son of one of Silius' colleagues in Germany and bore Silius a grudge from those days. Not only that, but when Silius objected to this biased prosecutor who was protected by his office, he incurred the impatience of Tiberius, who argued, with an irrelevant reference to republican precedent, that the consuls had a duty to defend the state against its enemies. In this way, Tiberius demonstrated his blindness to the fact that it was he, and not the consuls, who had a duty to protect the state. Thus Sejanus' manipulation of particular aspects of this case enabled him to blind Tiberius to the real issue, and, importantly, to make it look as if the attack on Silius emanated from Tiberius himself. This was bound to convince Agrippina that it was Tiberius, rather than Sejanus, who was orchestrating the attack on her and her friends. Silius anticipated condemnation by committing suicide.

In AD 26, an attack was launched upon Agrippina's cousin, Claudia Pulchra. Again, she saw Tiberius as responsible, and rather pointedly chided him for attacking the descendants of Augustus. Any imputation that Tiberius was demeaning Augustus' memory was bound to anger the *princeps*; he in his turn accused Agrippina of envy solely because she did not enjoy power and influence. Another example of Sejanus' planning is to be seen in his success in convincing both Tiberius and Agrippina that each was trying to poison the other; skilfully, because of their isolation, he was able to pose as the trustworthy confidant of each of them.

During these years, Sejanus also tried to advance his cause by seeking Tiberius' permission to marry his mistress, the widowed Livilla. Sejanus clearly had two motives for such a marriage. First, it would have brought him into the family of the *princeps* and given him some quasi-parental control over Tiberius' grandson, Tiberius Gemellus. Second, a new marriage for Livilla was bound to heighten Agrippina's isolation and sense of vulnerability. Tiberius recognised that this would be the effect but not that it was Sejanus' intention. Although he did not forbid the marriage, he made it clear that he did not favour it.

By this time, Tiberius was growing increasingly weary of the cares of office, and looking towards withdrawing from Rome. In Tacitus' view, it was an incident in one particular trial which pushed Tiberius into his decision to retire: he was forced to listen to a witness, who was probably hand-picked by Sejanus, recounting singularly unpleasant remarks about Tiberius, alleged to have been made by the accused. Although Tacitus introduces a number of possible reasons for Tiberius' decision to withdraw to Capreae, he recognised Sejanus' intrigues as the principal force. Sejanus' plan was that the retired emperor would be entirely dependent on him for loyal service and indeed even for information. Sejanus intended effectively to be the censor of news to and from Capreae; he hoped too that, with Tiberius away from Rome, he would have a freer hand to promote his scheme of undermining Agrippina, her family and friends. At the same time, it would be easier to ensure that the blame for what he did actually fell upon Tiberius. By chance, Sejanus was at a crucial moment able to reinforce Tiberius' trust in and dependence on him, when he saved the life of the *princeps* during a rockfall at a cave at Sperlonga (near Naples).

With Tiberius remote and introspective on Capreae, Sejanus had a freer hand to accelerate his plans against Agrippina; he singled out particularly her eldest son, Nero, for harassment and intimidation, and was even able to work upon the jealousies that existed between Nero and his brother, Drusus, using the latter to spy upon Nero. His clandestine methods brought the added advantage of leaving Agrippina extremely uncertain as to who were her friends and who were her enemies, particularly since Sejanus continued to pose as her friend. This state of affairs had an important consequence in the aftermath of Sejanus' fall in AD 31; for many on Agrippina's side, including Agrippina herself, found it difficult, if not impossible, to convince the hyper-suspicious Tiberius that they were not in some way associated with Sejanus. Indeed, even whilst Sejanus was still in favour, Tiberius is said to have become sensitive to the apparent connections between Sejanus and some of Agrippina's friends, including, prominently, Tiberius' old rival, Asinius Gallus.

In AD 28, another of Agrippina's friends, Titius Sabinus, was judicially attacked in a case that presented a particularly unedifying example of spying and information collection, but in which the accusers emphasised a real and strong connection between treachery and Agrippina's group. The ground was by now prepared for the launching of an attack on Agrippina herself; events moreover, played into Sejanus' hands through the death in AD 29 of the octogenarian Livia. Although no friend of Agrippina, her presence in Rome did, the sources imply, exercise some element of restraining control over Sejanus. As a result of the attack, Agrippina, Nero, Drusus and a number of their supporters were incarcerated; Nero committed suicide in prison in AD 30.

The course of events over the following year is far from clear, but from a position in which few Romans of any class of society would dare incur his wrath, Sejanus fell to disgrace and his death on 18 October, AD 31, following the reading in the senate of what Juvenal, the satiric poet, called the 'long and wordy letter from Capreae'. The reason for the difficulty in understanding these events stems from the fact that the text of Tacitus' *Annals* is lost for this period. As a result, it is not clear what Sejanus was planning in these last months of his life, or why Tiberius turned on and destroyed him.

Tiberius himself is said to have stated in his own autobiography that he destroyed Sejanus because of the latter's plots against the children of Germanicus. Little serious consideration, however, has ever been given to this claim because Sejanus' fall brought no alleviation for Agrippina, for her second son, Drusus, nor for Agrippina's friend, Asinius Gallus. However, we should bear in mind that some time in AD 30, apparently on the advice of Antonia, his sister-in-law, Tiberius had Gaius Caligula and his sisters moved from Rome to Capreae – perhaps to offer them improved protection. Also Tacitus records that in the wake of Sejanus' fall, a charge was brought against at least one man of having been Sejanus' accomplice in his plots against Caligula.

Further, the deaths of Agrippina, Drusus and Asinius Gallus are less damaging to Tiberius' version of events than might at

47

first sight appear. When Drusus died in AD 33, Tiberius launched a savage posthumous attack on him for the damage he had done to Rome and to his family; we should recall that Sejanus had enlisted the help of the uncongenial Drusus in bringing about the ruin of his unsuspecting brother, Nero. Tiberius might then justifiably have regarded Drusus as an accomplice of Sejanus. Again, when Agrippina died on 18 October, AD 33, Tiberius took some satisfaction in noting the coincidence that it was two years to the day from Sejanus' own death. Sejanus' strategy of appearing to befriend Agrippina may in retrospect have left some suspicion in Tiberius' mind of an association between her and Sejanus; he had, after all, come to see both as bent on his own destruction. Finally, in the case of Asinius Gallus, Tiberius had long suspected this long-serving senator of trying to undermine him; Dio Cassius reports a rather strange accusation which Tiberius made against Gallus – that he was trying to 'steal' Sejanus from him. This would indicate that Tiberius suspected a liaison between the two. In any case, so many senators had tried to ingratiate themselves with Sejanus that there must have been many of Agrippina's friends who had made contacts with Sejanus which in the aftermath of the prefect's fall must have been very hard to explain.

There is, then, no insurmountable objection to accepting Tiberius' own explanation of Sejanus' fall. Indeed the prefect's continued attacks on Agrippina and her family would, if successfully completed, have left only Gemellus and his mother, Livilla; if Sejanus had been successful in his effort to marry Livilla, he would have been left as the guardian of Tiberius' sole surviving heir – surely an unassailable position. It is also clear that during AD 30 and 31 Sejanus tried to build further support for himself – amongst the *plebs* of Rome and amongst the armies; it seems that he had made approaches to the commanders of the armies in both Upper and Lower Germany. Such troops would have supported him not perhaps in a plot against Tiberius, for which there is no good evidence, but in the fluid situation that might have followed Tiberius' death. However, it would seem that Sejanus' best chance of continued advancement lay with Tiberius remaining *princeps* until his natural death.

The fact that Tiberius was evidently put on his guard against Sejanus in AD 30 but took no action until close to the end of AD

31 indicates that the *princeps* perceived no immediate danger emanating from Sejanus; he could afford to play a waiting game.

The year AD 31 opened with Tiberius and Sejanus as consuls, Tiberius rarely held the consulate during his reign, and Sejanus evidently expected that a consulate with Tiberius as his colleague indicated the likelihood of promotion for himself – perhaps a grant of tribunician power along with the *princeps*, or permission at last for his marriage to Livilla. In the event, Tiberius resigned his consulship in May, having given no indication of new favour – an omission which must surely have caused Sejanus to doubt the security of his position. Indeed, it may have been fear of what Sejanus might do out of desperation that led Tiberius secretly to instruct that, in the event of an armed insurrection, the young Drusus Caesar should be released from prison and established as a kind of emergency figurehead for the Caesars.

As it turned out, nothing went awry; Tiberius took few people into his confidence beyond Sertorius Macro (Sejanus' replacement as prefect) and the consul, Memmius Regulus. The letter of denunciation was evidently equivocal in tone until the last moment, and Sejanus until then appears to have continued expecting to hear of his long-awaited promotion. In the event, nobody stood on ceremony; the prefect was dragged off to his death, whilst, according to Juvenal's masterly description, the people threw themselves into destroying Sejanus' statues with as much zest as they had shown in his support only hours before.

Sejanus' death was followed by a witch-hunt for anyone who was suspected of having supported him; few could escape the inference, though the accusers must have used the highly charged atmosphere to bring down many whose crimes were no greater than that of the *princeps* himself. After all, so long as Tiberius trusted Sejanus there would have seemed no good reason for anyone to act otherwise. Sejanus' family was treated with especial violence, and his estranged wife Apicata at last told the full story of her husband's relationship with Livilla. Whilst such evidence as she gave should have been treated with caution, the revelation of Sejanus' murder of Drusus would have hit Tiberius hard, further exacerbating the bitterness and disillusion he was feeling already.

Whilst we cannot be certain how far Sejanus' approaches to

49

army commanders had proceeded, the whole episode – particularly with the concentration of the praetorian guard within Rome itself – would have highlighted the extreme sensitivity of the relationship between the *princeps* and the army. There were of course special reasons why Tiberius became so dependent upon Sejanus – the isolation forced upon Tiberius by his age, his character, his unpopularity, his poor relationships with members of his family. However, whilst few emperors would have gone so far as to call their prefects 'partner of my labours', few either would have risked antagonising such a potentially powerful servant. It was with good reason that the emperor Vespasian (AD 69–79) later experimented with locating the prefecture within his own family.

The legacy of Sejanus was the near-destruction of the imperial family, the accelerated sycophancy of the senatorial order, and a *princeps* who could never again face returning from an exile to which Sejanus' machinations had consigned him. The legacy of Sejanus' fall was fear and suspicion amongst the nobility, and a new prefect who, if anything, was more cruel, depraved and power-hungry than Aelius Sejanus himself.

7

Tiberius and the Empire

Shortly before Augustus' death in AD. 14 he had allegedly instructed his successor not to engage in imperialist adventures but to retain the Empire within its existing frontiers. Some regarded this as the words of a *princeps* jealous of his own reputation being surpassed; in reality, the recent Varus disaster had highlighted the delicate balance which existed between the size of the army and the fulfilment of current garrison duties. In short, without an enlargement of the army, which would have been politically and economically risky, the possibility of imperial expansion was minimal. The trauma of the Varus disaster had left a healthy respect for those who faced the legions across the frontiers.

It is unlikely in any case that Augustus' advice seriously conflicted with Tiberius' natural inclinations. His own military reputation was that of a cautious commander, and it was of course he who in the decade before his accession had had to cope with both the Pannonian rebellion (AD 6–9) and the Varus disaster itself in AD 9. In any case, the Rhine army was clearly still, in AD 14, in an uncertain state because of the programme of crash-recruitment that had been necessary to restore its numbers after AD 9. The simultaneous mutinies in AD 14 on both the Rhine and the Danube provided a sober warning that much still needed to be done before the legionary army was again worthy of its reputation. Circumstances and inclination therefore pointed Tiberius Caesar in the same direction.

Such considerations made Tiberius' principate an unusually inactive period from the military point of view; as Tacitus noted, this gave the historian particular problems in his account of the reign. Historians of Rome produced their works initially for a listening audience, and Tiberius' principate lacked the dramatic military episodes which lent embellishment and colour to the historian's production. It was probably the artist's reaction which led to Tacitus' dismissive description of a 'peace that was not disturbed' and a '*princeps* uninterested in imperial expansion'.

None the less, the reign had its share of military and imperial problems, although the warfare between AD 14 and 37 was for the most part reactive, and concerned with preventing disturbance to the prosperous development of provinces. Of such a kind was the lengthy war against the guerrilla leader, Tacfarinas, in north Africa (AD 17–24); though ultimately Roman success was not in doubt, it was not won without political embarrassment over the choice of Sejanus' uncle, Quintus Junius Blaesus, to command the war.

In AD 21–2, the Rhine legions had to be mobilised to deal with a 'nationalist' outbreak in Gaul; the name of one of its leaders, Julius Sacrovir ('Holy man'), suggests that the tribal nationalism may have been inspired by druidic priests, displaying the same blend of patriotism and religious fervour which Caesar had seen in Britain nearly a century before. Since both its leaders bore the Roman name of Julius, indicating their enfranchisement, this outbreak highlighted the dangers of nationalism which might in the relatively early days of a province's development be concealed behind a façade of romanisation and waiting to be provoked by high-handed behaviour on the part of Roman officials. This war too had political overtones in Rome, since Sejanus was able to utilise for his own ends jealousy between the Roman commanders involved, Visellius Varro and Gaius Silius, who was a friend of Germanicus and Agrippina. The client-kingdom of Thrace was also disturbed and required an armed intervention in AD 26 to secure the position of Rhoemetalces, the pro-Roman occupant of the Thracian throne.

The Rhine and the east, Rome's most sensitive frontier areas,

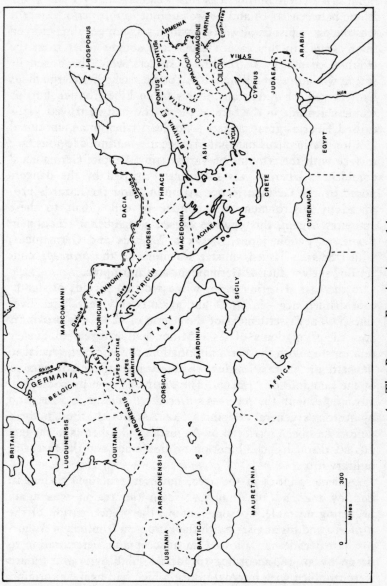

4 The Roman Empire in AD 14

both saw action during Tiberius' reign. Activity east of the Rhine between AD 14 and 16 was unique in this period, since it was the only episode of warfare which was not genuinely forced upon Rome. In this case, Germanicus sought relief from the troubles of mutiny in the cheap success which he hoped he would win across the Rhine. It is not clear whether Germanicus had revived the Augustan dreams of an Elbe frontier, but his reckless attitude in the face of those who had destroyed Varus caused Tiberius great anxiety – not least when in an emotional mission Germanicus brought his recently-mutinous legions face to face with the remains of Varus' army. Despite Germanicus' confidence, Tiberius was sufficiently worried by the dangers posed by the German leader, Arminius, and the hazards produced by environment and climate to call a halt to these activities. Again, this episode caused a significant reaction in Rome, as people judged between Tiberius and Germanicus, whilst Sejanus issued sinister warnings to the *princeps* concerning the conduct of Germanicus and Agrippina.

In the east, Tiberius' reign witnessed two periods of significant disturbance – in AD 16 and again twenty years later. Ever since Pompey's settlement of the region in 62 BC, the provinces and client-kingdoms of Asia Minor had enjoyed an uneasy relationship with the Parthian kingdom to their east; crucial to the state of this relationship was the stance of the government of the kingdom of Armenia. The Parthians won psychological advantages with the reverses suffered by Crassus in 53 BC and by Antony's general, Decidius Saxa, in 36 BC, though these defeats had been retrieved by Augustus and Tiberius in the late 20s BC, through a combination of diplomacy and the threat of military force.

Dynastic politics in the area, however, remained turbulent, and by the end of Augustus' reign the region was again becoming unstable. To some extent, the preoccupation of the *princeps* and his advisers with the European frontiers in Augustus' last decade had allowed an unacceptable deterioration to occur. By AD 16, according to Tacitus, both Syria and Judaea were troubled with internal unrest which had financial origins, and the client-kingdoms of Cilicia, Cappadocia and Commagene had vacant thrones. Most serious of all, Vonones, the pro-Roman king of Parthia, had been driven from the kingdom by Artabanus but, much to Artabanus' annoyance, had been accepted on to the throne of Armenia. Vonones, however, under pressure, had fled, leaving the Armenian throne vacant also.

As always, Tiberius preferred a diplomatic solution; so, following Augustan precedent, he sent to the area his heir, Germanicus Caesar, whom, according to Tacitus, he was glad to be able to prise away from the Rhine legions. The political repercussions in Rome of Germanicus' mission and of his disastrous relationship with Cnaeus Piso, the governor of Syria, have already been discussed (see Chapter 5 p. 38). However, the mission successfully stabilised Asia Minor; Commagene was made into a province, whilst new kings were settled on the thrones of Cappadocia and Cilicia. Further, Germanicus installed the durable Zeno (Artaxias) as king of Armenia, and he was to retain the position until his death in AD 34 or 35. This brought stability and reduced any threat from Parthia; in the main, Rome had by this time lost any taste for intervention in Parthia and preferred to leave the area to dynastic squabbling.

However, the death of Zeno precipitated new disturbance, possibly promoted on the part of Artabanus, the Parthian king, in the expectation that the old and reclusive emperor would be slow to respond. He placed his son, Arsaces, on the throne of Armenia, and demanded that Tiberius surrender a considerable amount of territory in Asia Minor. A diplomatic solution was again achieved, on this occasion through the agency of Lucius Vitellius, the newly appointed, youthful governor of Syria. It says a great deal for Tiberius' continued sharpness on major issues that he could make such an imaginative appointment.

Thus, Tiberius avoided direct intervention in the area, but rather manipulated the situation towards the conclusion he desired. He supported the pretensions to the Armenian throne of Mithridates of Iberia and caused Artabanus sufficient anxiety to bring him to heel; he thereby initiated another period of stability in the region which lasted until shortly before the death of Claudius in AD 54. The Jewish historian, Josephus, informs us of an imaginative intervention by Vitellius in Judaea too, which led to the removal of the much despised procurator, Pontius Pilate.

In all, Tiberius' dealings with the eastern provinces and kingdoms showed firmness and imagination, which enabled the *princeps* on two occasions to secure effective solutions without recourse to major military intervention, thus honouring the spirit of Augustus' advice not to tamper unnecessarily with existing arrangements. In the day-to-day management of existing provinces, Tiberius' principate was acknowledged as a period in which high standards were sought and generally enforced; officials who overstepped the mark were usually dealt with firmly, and Tiberius' subsequent attitude to such people was generally hostile. Tacitus remarks on the maintenance of fair levels of taxation, and the observation of the *princeps* that 'my sheep should be clipped, not shaved' is well known. It was a wise policy, since restlessness over tax burdens complicated problems in the east, was at least a pretext for Sacrovir's rebellion in Gaul, and drove the Frisii of north Germany to a short, but violent, rebellion in AD 28.

Tiberius' commitment to high standards led him on one occasion to exclude Gaius Galba, the brother of the future emperor, from participation in the drawing of lots for proconsulships, on the ground that he had squandered his inheritance; presumably it was feared that he might seek to rebuild his fortune at the expense of his province. Further, the view of the *princeps* that, if given long periods of office, governors might be less tempted to corrupt practices is adduced as a possible explanation for the extremely lengthy governorships enjoyed by some – most notably Poppaeus Sabinus, who remained in charge of Moesia and the Greek provinces for twenty-four years.

Tiberius' provincial appointments were generally sound; the few exceptions stand out in sharp contrast, such as Cnaeus Piso in Syria (AD 17–20), Pontius Pilate in Judaea (AD 26–36), Gaius Silius in Germany (AD 14–21). Increasing concern was also shown over the behaviour of governors' wives during their husbands' provincial appointments; whilst Tiberius may have been particularly concerned with the exceptional case of Agrippina, he clearly recognised a more general problem, as is shown by his attitude to Plancina (wife of Cnaeus Piso), Sosia Galla (wife of Gaius Silius), and the wife of Pomponius Labeo in Moesia. The onus of responsibility was placed on their husbands' shoulders by the enactment that offences committed in the provinces by officials' wives would be treated as if they had been committed by the husbands themselves.

Tiberius was strict rather than innovative, preferring to stay with well-tried methods. We should, however, mention the rather curious cases of two governors, Aelius Lamia (Syria) and

Lucius Arruntius (Spain), who were appointed but apparently not permitted to go to their provinces. Suetonius even says that their deputies were given the instructions relevant to the governing of their provinces, which tends to argue against Tacitus' explanation that Tiberius had forgotten that he had made the appointments. It is unlikely that the *princeps* felt that he had any need to doubt the loyalty of the two individuals concerned, and the possibility remains that these cases were experimental in the sense that the 'departmental head' was being kept in Rome where he could be directly and immediately answerable to the *princeps* on questions relating to his province. If, however, this does represent 'cabinet government' in embryonic form, then the experiment did not proceed; only one other case is known during the early principate – a governor of Syria who was retained in Rome by Nero.

The distinction between imperial and senatorial provinces was generally maintained, although Tiberius might interfere to secure good government. Normally, he encouraged the senate to exercise a proper responsibility for its provinces and officials, and tried to halt the apparently growing practice of governors of senatorial provinces filing their reports with him rather than with the senate. He also showed irritation when the senate referred to him provincial matters which he regarded as being within its proper competence (see p. 28).

Tiberius did not make extraordinary demands of Rome's provincial subjects; he did not require 'worship' of himself. Indeed, he reined in what he regarded as extravagant requests. Tacitus recounts his refusal of the request made by the people of Hispania Ulterior to be permitted to set up a shrine to himself and Livia. The *princeps* pointed out correctly that cases quoted by the Spaniards as precedents were in fact inappropriate since Augustan practice had been to combine worship of the *princeps* with that of the personified **Roma**, and Augustus himself had previously acceded to a request only because it combined worship of himself with that of the senate. Characteristically, Tiberius felt bound to follow Augustan precedent in the matter but was resolved to stop short of condoning flattery which he felt would only devalue the honours already given to Augustus. The sentiments which Tacitus ascribes to Tiberius in his repudiation of the Spanish request are precisely echoed in a surviving letter which Tiberius wrote on the same subject to the Greek town of Gytheum. The monument which Tiberius desired above all was a reputation for having governed the Empire well.

As we have seen, he was certainly alert to the need for fair-minded and efficient officials, and we may assume that for most of his principate he was alert also to requests for advice and assistance, of the type referred to later in Pliny's correspondence with Trajan (AD 98–117) from the province of Bithynia. Surviving inscriptions show that, throughout his reign, Tiberius continued his predecessor's close care and attention to matters affecting the prosperity and well-being of provinces, even those most distant from Rome; in particular, road construction and public building were vigorously pursued. There is little evidence that this slackened in the later years, although a surviving rescript of Claudius' reign concerning the status of certain Alpine communities indicates that Claudius was solving a problem which had been neglected because of his 'uncle's persistent absence'.

Tiberius responded generously to natural disasters in the provinces, as is shown dramatically by the grants of money and remission of taxes which were made to twelve cities of Asia devastated by an earthquake in AD 17. This act of generosity, which was commemorated on the coinage, was the cause of the request, which Tiberius granted, that his generosity be acknowledged through the dedication of a temple to him at Smyrna.

As was so often the case with Rome's early emperors, Tiberius' unpopularity in Rome contrasts strongly with his reputation in the provinces. He may not have had the same vision as Caesar and Augustus of an empire bound together by rapidly rising provincial status and self-esteem; indeed, presiding as he did over a period which saw little warfare or territorial expansion, he may not have appreciated the socio-political necessity of enhancing the status of provincials. He did, however, have a traditional, 'patronal' interest in the prosperity of his subjects, which, though it may not have appealed to the more progressive instincts of an emperor such as Claudius, none the less secured the appreciation of the subject-populations. Tiberius was viewed in the provinces as a monarch anxious for their well-being and alert to the actions which would secure this.

8

Tiberius' retirement from Rome: his later years

In AD 26, Tiberius left Rome, ostensibly to dedicate temples in Campania. However, from there he went across to Capreae, taking up a retirement in the Villa Iovis; he never returned to Rome. Contemporary and subsequent generations, because they could not understand the reasons for this retirement, have surrounded it with speculation, often of the most malevolent kind. Yet, as we have seen (in Chapter 7), many of the policies and actions of Tiberius in the Empire which have been seen as sound, even inspired, date from this period. It is clear, therefore, that whatever the reasons for and the course of that retirement, Tiberius Caesar did not lose his grip on affairs.

There was, of course, nothing extraordinary in a member of Rome's nobility having a villa in southern Italy. The Bay of Naples had been the site of numerous luxurious retreats ever since the last century of the republic. Augustus had a number of such villas, including perhaps twelve on Capreae, named after the gods of the pantheon of Olympus. The Villa Iovis (Villa of Jove) was perhaps the finest of these, situated on a rocky and almost unapproachable headland at the eastern end of the island.

By the standards of villas depicted on wall-paintings at Pompeii and Herculaneum, or castigated for their exotic architecture by the poet Horace (Quintus Horatius Flaccus), the Villa Iovis was not out of the ordinary. It consisted of suites of rooms

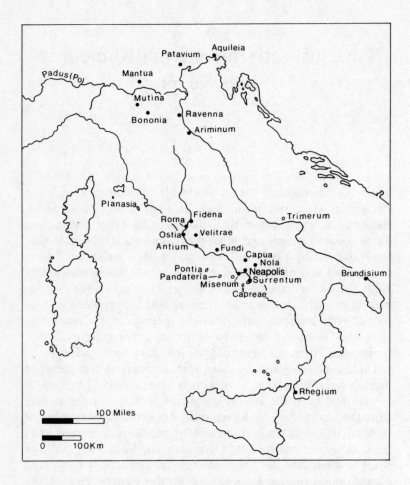

Padus (Po)

Patavium **Aquileia**

Mantua

Mutina

Bononia **Ravenna**

Ariminum

Planasia

Fidena **Trimerum**

Roma

Ostia **Velitrae**

Antium

Fundi

Capua

Nola

Pontia **Neapolis**

Pandateria **Surrentum** **Brundisium**

Misenum

Capreae

0   100 Miles

0   100 Km

Rhegium

5   Map of Italy

on each of four sides of a square courtyard. Architecturally, the most remarkable features are the huge vaulted water-cisterns beneath this courtyard, and the numerous ramps and staircases necessitated by the uneven nature of the terrain on which the villa was built. The grounds contained some conceits, such as a summer dining-room, but otherwise the site is essentially modest, and, apart from its remoteness of approach from land and sea, has little to fuel the speculation about Tiberius' use of it.

The reasons for the retirement have been summarised by Tacitus. He believed that the principal reason was pressure exerted on the *princeps* by Sejanus. Yet Tacitus observed a collection of other factors which pointed the *princeps* in the direction in which Sejanus was pushing him. In the first place, he was growing increasingly sensitive about his reputation for cruelty and sexual perversion. It was perhaps inevitable that such a construction should have been placed on the activities of a man who was by nature isolated and reclusive. Indeed, Tiberius already had such a reputation before he became *princeps*, for on an earlier occasion (in 6 BC), his sense of frustration had led him to seek a physical isolation on the island of Rhodes (see Chapter 2, p. 11). It is undoubtedly true that Tiberius was sensitive to such gossip, as is shown by his outburst during the trial of Votienus Montanus shortly before (see p. 46); as we have seen, it is not unlikely that the course of that trial was deliberately engineered by Sejanus, who probably primed a crucial witness to make the maximum impact upon the *princeps*. The result of it was said to have been a determination on Tiberius' part to cut himself off from the senate. However, the company which he took with him into retirement does little to confirm such suspicions; besides Sejanus, this included two old friends, Cocceius Nerva and Curtius Atticus, and teachers with whom he could relax. For Tiberius the most important member of the company, as on Rhodes, was probably the astrologer, Thrasyllus, with whom no doubt the *princeps* pondered the frustrations of the past and looked morbidly to the future. This is clearly shown by the much-quoted preface of a letter which he wrote from Capreae to the senate, displaying a preoccupation with failure, guilt and retribution: 'If I know what to write to you, senators, or how to write it, or what not to write, may heaven plunge me into a worse ruin than I feel overtaking me each day.'

A second problem concerned the physical appearance of the *princeps*. Although not necessarily a truthful guide, Tiberius' coin-portraits and sculptural representations show him as a tall and good-looking man, with no features which would obviously cause great sensitivity. It does seem, however, that he was suffering from a skin complaint which had unsightly consequences, and which both ancient and modern medical opinion has seen in the light of an 'epidemic' current at the time, rather than as something peculiar to the *princeps*.

Tacitus also mentions Tiberius' relationship with his aged mother, Livia, as a cause of his decision to retire; she is said to have harassed him, particularly reminding him of the debt which she claimed he owed her for her services over his elevation. She stated that it was due solely to her efforts that Augustus had eventually preferred Tiberius to Germanicus as his successor. It is quite likely that by AD 26 Tiberius' weariness with the problems of his office had left him less than grateful for her efforts; in any case, however, as Tacitus observed in another context, services are welcome only so long as they are capable of repayment.

Even at the opening of his principate, Tiberius had expressed an interest in the possibility that he might one day be relieved of the burdens of office. Although much of the domestic and foreign administration had functioned smoothly, he clearly found his duties increasingly wearisome, particularly in the light of the treason trials and especially because of the constant difficulties in his relationship first with Germanicus and subsequently with his widow. In AD 26, Tiberius was nearing 70 years of age; death had removed many of his older friends, leaving him increasingly isolated. He had already indicated how welcome it was to have Sejanus as his partner, and it must have seemed logical for Sejanus' share of the workload to increase as time passed by.

However, it is clear that in some ways the retirement did him no good at all, as all the energy which had previously been used in his conscientious attention to his duties was now devoted to credulous and malignant suspicions which Sejanus deliberately encouraged. Unable to stand company, yet unable to handle the solitude, Tiberius had subsided into a state of cringing withdrawal. More than once he came to the mainland and spent considerable periods in residence in his villas around the Bay of

Naples; yet he could not steel himself to return to Rome itself. It is an indication of Tacitus' appreciation of the mental state of the *princeps* that he used the word *abscessus* ('cowering departure') to describe the retirement, rather than *absentia*, which would more properly be used of a passive state of absence.

In one sense, the retirement from Rome indicated a governmental crisis; a prerequisite of the Augustan principate was the active participation of the *princeps* in the deliberations of the senate, which had in the past felt peculiarly powerless if left to its own devices. Both Augustus and Tiberius prior to AD 26 had been present for debates, able to answer and to contribute, even to veto when necessary. In place of this active participation, imperial orders contained in letters were substituted, which many senators found more intimidating than the imperial presence and which certainly seemed to admit of much less dissent.

More immediately, the power of Sejanus was increased; Tiberius heard only what Sejanus wanted him to hear, and the prefect clearly had great scope to pursue his designs with less fear of being checked or rebuked by Tiberius. Similarly, it was easy for Sejanus to make sure that the full odium for his actions should fall upon Tiberius himself and thus to sever the *princeps* more completely from those who might have saved him from Sejanus. For example, although the campaign to destroy Agrippina and her family was ultimately the work of Sejanus, few would have placed the blame for it anywhere but on the shoulders of the *princeps*.

The retirement from public contact generated its own mythology, and it is now impossible to tell what credence should be placed in the stories of Tiberius' perversions and extravagances; there were certainly those who, like Suetonius, were active in compiling them. Yet, whilst some of the stories tell of Tiberius' cruelty, more indicate his exasperation if the privacy of his retreat was invaded; he guarded his solitude with great jealousy. We lack detailed evidence for his state of mind in the early years of retirement, and most of what survives concerns the period after the fall of Sejanus in AD 31, when the *princeps* was devoured with frustration and disillusion, and fanatically suspicious of anyone – and there were many – who might have had a link with Sejanus; 58 per cent of the major judicial proceedings recorded during Tiberius' reign occurred between AD 31 and the death of the *princeps* in March, AD 37.

Yet, despite his desire to have a clear distance imposed between himself and his subjects, Tiberius was throughout this last period of his life clearly abreast of events in the outside world, and capable of handling them firmly and fairly. If, as seems likely, he was aware of the perfidy of Sejanus for at least eighteen months before he administered the *coup de grâce*, he was certainly capable of maintaining a consistent deception throughout that period. Further, the moves he made with regard to Germanicus' daughters and his youngest son indicate a firm grasp of his duty as emperor and, in settling the daughters in respectable marriages with members of the senatorial nobility, a firm and imaginative grasp also of his duty as a substitute parent. The careful arrangement of events which terminated in Sejanus' fall shows a clarity of thinking and planning which contrasts markedly with the uncritical fears which he displayed in the face of those who might have been involved with Sejanus.

He was capable too of prompt and fair-minded action in the face of national disaster. After his decision to quit Rome, three major disasters found him as attentive to his subjects' interests as he had been at the time of the Asian earthquake in AD 17. Following the collapse of the amphitheatre at Fidenae in AD 27, he actively encouraged people to come to the aid of those affected. In the wake of a financial crisis in AD 33, in which strict enforcement of the usury laws had led to a great deal of harsh privation and loss of confidence, he made a large sum of treasury money available to relieve the immediate distress and allow time for confidence to return. Again, in AD 36, following a disastrous fire on the Aventine Hill in Rome, the *princeps* showed great generosity and established a commission to investigate the losses properly. Such a combination of generosity and prudence had always been a characteristic of Tiberius.

As we have seen (in Chapter 7), the great issues of foreign policy also found him alert, even imaginative, in his reactions; his handling of the renewed difficulties in the east in AD 34, through the agency of Lucius Vitellius, was little short of masterly.

Tiberius' fears and suspicions in these last years led to many trials, convictions and suicides as some people exploited the opportunities these provided. Others despaired of the state of

Tiberius' government. Yet the *princeps* showed himself capable of perceptiveness in small matters as well as large: he could still, as in his younger days, see through a malicious prosecution and bring relief to an accused person. He was still capable of seeing where idle suspicions were misplaced, as in the case of the talented Cornelius Gaetulicus who, as commander of the Upper German legions, was suspected by some of complicity with Sejanus.

But, if we certainly cannot charge Tiberius with a wholesale neglect of his duties during the last decade of his life, and if we can see signs of alertness and attention, clearly all was not well, as the frequency of trials and suicides of men who, like Cocceius Nerva and Lucius Arruntius, were old associates of the *princeps*, shows. Tiberius was inconsistent, veering from perceptiveness, fairness and generosity to doubt, gloom and suspicion. Few could tell how he might react in any particular circumstance; the ease with which vague suspicions might lead to trial and death will have left many pondering their futures with grave anxiety. This anxiety, which removed the last vestiges of spirit from the nobility, was the real cancer of Tiberius' last years. Yet those who could apply cool thought to his reign, and assess it in its entirety, would have seen that such inconsistency and credulity had always been aspects of the principate of Tiberius Caesar.

In spite of his experience and maturity, Tiberius had shown himself throughout his reign as incapable of withstanding the pressures of office. For Tiberius Caesar this was the legacy of the deified Augustus; the price which Tiberius paid was a tortured life as *princeps* and, despite the many positive aspects of his reign, a public esteem so low that when the *princeps* died on 16 March, AD 37, at the age of 78, he was consigned to rapid oblivion. Rome turned with relief and anticipation to the rising star, Gaius Caligula, the youngest son of Germanicus.

9

The succession

Tiberius' own succession to the principate had been unexpected; throughout his life, Augustus had shown a strong inclination to be succeeded by a member of his own – the Julian – family. Tiberius' own emergence had been the result of premature deaths amongst Augustus' preferred nominees. Finally, in AD 4, despite the fact that Augustus was said to have been inclined in favour towards his granddaughter's husband, Germanicus, he decided to place his ultimate succession hopes upon Tiberius. Even so, the hopes of the Julian family were kept alive through Augustus' instruction to Tiberius that his heir should be Germanicus (whom he was required to adopt as his son) in preference to his own son, Drusus.

Germanicus, of course, died in AD 19, but there is every indication that Tiberius intended to honour the spirit of Augustus' wishes. Drusus was, it is true, given a grant of tribunician power in AD 21, but there is some evidence to suggest that, as in Tiberius' own case in 6 BC, this was to equip him better to act as a present helper and guardian of the real heirs. Drusus was to safeguard the interests of Nero and Drusus, the sons of Germanicus, presumably as they were prepared for the likelihood of power. Tiberius' decision in AD 23, after Drusus' death, to entrust the two boys to the care of the senate suggests that he continued to take their future elevation seriously. It is equally evident that Sejanus' motive in organising Drusus' murder was to ensure that Tiberius' heirs were left in a dangerously exposed position.

Despite his continued expectation of their promotion, Tiberius was unwilling to see this happen too swiftly: for example, in AD 24, he strongly rebuked the priests for including Nero and Drusus within the new year's prayers for the emperor's safety. His warning that they might be ruined by such premature adulation was not the excuse that it is sometimes alleged to have been, but represents real anxiety based on his own unhappy memories as a stepfather responsible for Gaius and Lucius Caesar.

Sejanus' plans were based upon the elimination of the sons of Germanicus from consideration for the succession. Because of his withdrawal from the centre of political life in Rome, Tiberius denied himself access to the truth of this until after it was too late to save Nero; further, he came to understand the deadly role that the young Drusus had played in the removal of his brother. The *princeps* refused reconciliation with Drusus, though he did temporarily acknowledge his possible usefulness during the working-out of his own plans to trap and ruin Sejanus. Tiberius took seriously the damage done by Sejanus to the children of Germanicus; as we have seen, he ensured the safety of Caligula and his sisters, and encouraged the prosecution of at least one man, Sextius Paconianus, for the part that he was alleged to have played in Sejanus' plots against Caligula.

Although in his last years Tiberius was still alert and capable of statesmanlike responses to major matters of state, it is less clear how actively he pondered the succession question. By AD 33, two serious candidates remained – Caligula and Tiberius Gemellus, the surviving grandson of the *princeps*. Tiberius' assessments of these two are not clear, though he may have recognised the destructiveness of Caligula and sought to safeguard his grandson by not pushing him forward as either the equal or the superior of Caligula. It is similarly possible that he looked towards Caligula for positive reasons – namely that he represented the last opportunity to honour the spirit of the intentions which Augustus had made clear in AD 4. Alternatively, it could be that Tiberius, who had often (though not always) baulked at seeming to usurp the senate's authority, did not wish to impose either of the young men upon the *respublica* and did not go beyond making arrangements for the disposal of his own property. In this case, Caligula's elevation would have owed much to the support of Sertorius Macro, the new praetorian prefect.

Whatever Tiberius' views on the succession, he did not provide Caligula with any of the 'apprenticeship' which he himself had served under Augustus. In AD 33, he received a quaestorship and a priesthood, which may have been an indication of the intentions of the *princeps*; beyond that, however, Tiberius seems to have done nothing but to provide Caligula with a companion in the person of the Jewish prince, Herod Agrippa, who could hardly have offered Caligula much of a training in the delicate business of the management of the principate.

It is unclear how far Caligula was maligned by the stories that were circulated about life with the reclusive *princeps*, though Tacitus records him as a faithful mirror of Tiberius' moods – 'never a better slave or a worse master'. It is said that a praetorian senator, Sextus Vistilius, was 'excluded from the emperor's friendship' for criticisms made about Caligula's morals, and that the unfortunate Vistilius committed suicide as a result.

Tiberius is credited with many prescient observations on the likely nature of life in Rome under Caligula – that he was 'nursing a viper in Rome's bosom' and that Caligula would have 'all of Sulla's vices, and none of his virtues'. Lucius Arruntius, who committed suicide shortly before Tiberius' own death, did so because he saw no hope for Rome under a Caligula guided by Macro, a man whom Arruntius regarded as more dangerous than Sejanus.

In Tacitus' account, Tiberius finally was unable to make a choice between Gemellus and Caligula, though he is said to have recognised that Caligula would murder Gemellus, unable presumably to brook such a rival. Tiberius is even said to have given consideration to Claudius, and as a last resort to the passing of power to men outside the imperial family – rather as Augustus is once said to have done. However, Tiberius put the suggestion aside as likely to bring contempt and humiliation to Augustus' memory and to the name of the Caesars. Macro at any rate assumed that Caligula was to be the next emperor; he was accused by Tiberius of deserting him for the 'rising sun'.

Tiberius was not spared rumour and gossip even in death.

There was a story that, assuming the aged *princeps* to be dead, Caligula had taken on the trappings of his new role, only to find that Tiberius had only fainted. Macro, showing his dependence on Caligula's success, rapidly smothered Tiberius to death to put the issue beyond doubt. Tiberius' death caused unrestrained joy in Rome; his subjects called for 'Tiberius to the Tiber', but they were soon to learn that 'the best day after a bad emperor is the first one'.

10
Conclusion

When Tacitus summarised Tiberius' life at the end of his account, he concentrated on the deterioration of Tiberius' personality, which he perceived as a gradual process in which the 'true character' of the *princeps* was revealed by stages. These were determined by Tiberius' relationship with various members of his family and entourage, and only after the death of Sejanus in AD 31 did his character become fully apparent.

Although the detail of Tacitus' analysis may be regarded as an artificial imposition, most commentators would attach considerable importance to Tiberius' personality. Tacitus reports anxieties which were entertained on this score even before Tiberius became *princeps*. Since Roman politics in the early Julio-Claudian period still revolved, as during the period of the old republic, around the relatively small circle of the senatorial nobility, the character of the leading member of that nobility is bound to have been of considerable significance. Tiberius and the senate were in almost daily contact and, as we have seen, how they reacted to each other could often be crucial. Tiberius' personality was such that the senate frequently did not know how it should react to him.

Most modern historians would consider Tacitus' character assessment as a significant part of the problem of understanding the principate of Tiberius, and, like Lucius Arruntius, would reflect upon the apparently destructive effect on this man of the exercise of supreme power. It should be recognised, however, that there were other elements necessary to an analysis of Tiberius' reign. These were to some extent reflected in the review which Tacitus conducted at the opening of *Annals* IV, at the halfway point in Tiberius' principate. Tacitus pointed to the essentially sound nature of much of the administration, though he reflected on the damaging effect of Tiberius' manner of conducting business.

An objective analysis would point to the fact that the principate devised by Augustus to suit his own circumstances was successfully transmitted to a successor even though Tiberius found the actual process traumatic. The new *princeps* demonstrated that the Augustan system could stand independently of its founder. Moreoever, the general soundness of Tiberius' administration allowed power to be transmitted again after his death – and to the part of the family that Augustus favoured. This might indicate that to a degree the senatorial nobility could regard the spirit of the old republic as still alive in a system where power was in the hands of the leading faction, but where theoretically it could pass to other factions and families. This is the true significance of the plan to 'restore the republic' at the time of the death of Caligula in AD 41. In other words, as Galba was later to point out, there was no inherent irreconcilability between *principatus* and *libertas* ('principate' and 'liberty').

There were during Tiberius' reign few major changes to the Augustan system; indeed Tiberius set great store by following Augustan precedents and principles. It is not clear whether this represented an obsession about Augustus, the conservatism of the new *princeps*, or even a genuine feeling that he was personally unworthy and no more than a 'caretaker' for the *gens Julia*.

The senate remained the main forum for the conduct of public business, and Tiberius may even have wished to enhance its powers; that he could not was partly the fault of the system and partly the result of his own lack of diplomacy in handling sensitive matters. The administration of the Empire was still exercised largely through senatorial agents, though senators may have felt restricted by their obvious lack of military opportunities. In truth, however, this was the legacy not so much of Tiberius as of the painful lessons of Augustus' last years. In this sense, those of our sources – and Tacitus may have been one of them – who knew of Hadrian's reign may have thought that they saw in the comparison between Augustus and Tiberius something similar to that between Trajan and Hadrian. Hadrian's generally non-expansionist approach made him unpopular in senatorial circles, even though his stewardship was generally sound and careful.

Tiberius' retirement to Capreae obviously cast the administration in a somewhat different light. He now depended less on discussion and more on imperial instruction. It is less clear how far this represented a change in the principle of the government or whether it was simply one of style. It did, however, demonstrate how the authority of a *princeps* could easily become the domination of a master – something which in his earlier days Tiberius would have attempted to avoid.

One change of this period which was of major significance for Tiberius himself and for the future of the principate concerned the role and organisation of the praetorian guard and its prefect. Tiberius dispensed with the dualism in the guard's command and acceded to Sejanus' arguments concerning the enhanced efficiency which would result from concentrating the guard into a single location. The logic of this argument would obviously appeal to a man of Tiberius' military experience, though the *princeps* lacked the judgement to be able to see through to Sejanus' intentions. The move certainly enabled Sejanus, when it mattered, to intimidate far more effectively.

Tiberius has been described as 'the victim of Augustus'. He certainly was so in the sense of being unable effectively to deploy the diplomacy that was an essential feature of Augustus' management technique; dissimulation, which Tacitus says was a virtue highly prized by Tiberius, was no substitute for diplomacy. Tiberius was also Augustus' victim in the matter of the dynastic aspirations of members of the Julian and Claudian families. Augustus had been ruthless in his use of his family and not least of Tiberius himself; his approach was direct and straightforward. Tiberius was never happy about his family relationships, and, unfortunately for him, those tensions that existed within the imperial family, which required Augustus' brand of directness, were not capable of being handled with the cold remoteness that was characteristic of Tiberius. Under these circumstances, ambitions went unchecked and unspoken suspicions abounded. The importance of this is ultimately that it provided a climate in which Sejanus' schemes could prosper.

The reign degenerated into fear, suspicion and recrimination; few would have rated the principate of Tiberius a success and few regretted his passing in AD 37, though even Caligula may have come to see that Tiberius was more often the victim than the perpetrator. A failure of communication led inevitably to the perceived failure of Tiberius' principate, despite the many sound features that attended it. Thus even his own modest anticipation of posterity's judgement was not to be fulfilled:

Senators, I am a human being, performing human tasks, and it is my ambition to fulfil the role of *princeps*. I want you to understand this, and I want future generations to believe it; you and they will do more than adequate service to my reputation if I am held to be worthy of my forebears, careful for your interests, steadfast in danger, and not afraid to be unpopular if I am serving the national good. As far as I am concerned, if you hold these opinions of me, they will stand as my temples and my finest statues, and they will last. For if posterity's judgement turns adversely, then stone structures are regarded as if they were the tombstones of people who do not deserve respect. So my prayer to the gods is that so long as I live they should grant me an easy conscience and a mind that knows its duty to gods and men. To provincials and Roman citizens, I pray that when I am dead my actions and reputation should be praised and well remembered.

[Tacitus, *Annals* IV. 38]

Tiberius was being sincere about his aspirations; it was a measure of his failure, however, that posterity has rarely been able to see him as he wished. Galba said later that a problem for emperors was the tendency of people to react to the emperor's position rather than to the emperor himself. Tiberius Caesar would not have disagreed.

Appendix I
The accounts of Tiberius' life and reign

Students of the reign of Tiberius are fortunate in the variety of surviving source material, though it represents of course only a small portion of what was written, which itself will have constituted the evidence upon which surviving accounts were based. Of the accounts of Tiberius' reign the most coherent is found in the first six books of the *Annals* of Cornelius Tacitus, which were written between *c*. AD 106 and 117. A near-contemporary of Tacitus was the biographer, Suetonius, whose *Life of Tiberius* was published probably in the 120s. Much later is the *Roman History* (written in Greek) of the Severan senator, Dio Cassius, who published his work probably in the 220s. Finally, a brief account, contemporary with Tiberius himself, was written by Velleius Paterculus, who published his work *c*. AD 30 – that is, before the disgrace and fall of Sejanus. Besides these, there are of course important references in other surviving writers, of which the most dramatic is the account of the fall of Sejanus in the tenth satire of Juvenal, another near-contemporary of Tacitus.

Obviously, these works have undergone close and lengthy scrutiny in an effort to determine their reliability and usefulness. Between the obsequious efforts of Velleius and the much more critical appraisals of Tacitus, Suetonius and Dio Cassius, it has been generally agreed that posterity has probably not been served particularly well; as Syme has put it, with reference to

Tacitus, those writing in the reigns of Trajan and Hadrian – that is, early in the second century AD – were probably 'blocked' in their efforts to reveal the truth by the 'consensus of educated opinion' (*Tacitus*, p. 421). In other words, an 'orthodox' view existed, which was hard to check, let alone correct.

Such a view may, however, be unduly pessimistic; despite Velleius' urgings to the contrary, we may assume from the absence of posthumous deification in Tiberius' case that the tradition of the unpopularity of the *princeps*, at least in senatorial circles, is generally correct. In any case, Tacitus shows in the introductory sections to both his *Histories* and his *Annals* that he was well aware of the pitfalls inherent in the accounts of earlier writers whose works he needed to consult: not only did the growing secrecy of the principate cloud issues and obscure the truth, but writers contemporary with their subjects were prone to fawn and flatter and those who, like Cremutius Cordus under Tiberius, did not could find their positions vulnerable to attack by those who played upon the fears and suspicions of the *princeps*. On the other hand, those who wrote later might display a liverish tendency which could easily be mistaken for a genuinely critical approach. The surviving account of Velleius certainly confirms the first part of Tacitus' observation.

The career of Velleius Paterculus was predominantly military; an equestrian officer who entered the senate after his election to the quaestorship in AD 7, he rose to the praetorship, along with his brother, in AD 15. This appears to have been the summit of his political progress, though, like many senators of praetorian standing, he may have enjoyed a number of subsequent provincial commissions. It is to be assumed that his writing, which was dedicated to Marcus Vinicius, consul in AD 30 and who in AD 33 was chosen by Tiberius as a husband for his granddaughter, Drusilla, was done mostly in the decade and a half between AD 15 and 30.

Velleius produced a compendium of Rome's history in two volumes and the nature of the work is far more personal than, for example, that of Tacitus. He was particularly interested in events in which he was involved, and, since he served alongside Tiberius on military campaigns prior to Tiberius' accession, he had come to know the future *princeps* in a context in which by all accounts he excelled. Tiberius is uncritically eulogised throughout the relevant sections, and it is a eulogy which was born of genuine admiration. Significantly, there is little (if any) falsification in Velleius' work; if the modern reader feels uncomfortable with the praise lavished upon both Tiberius and Sejanus, it should be remembered that Velleius was writing at a time when Sejanus was still in favour with the *princeps*, and of a period of which Tacitus too was broadly approving. From his distance, however, Tacitus could also recognise the effects of the grim demeanour of a *princeps* whom Velleius knew in a far more personal way. Indeed, the positive virtue of Velleius is the detail that comes from the immediacy which our other surviving sources lack.

Tacitus' senatorial career was far more impressive than that of Velleius; he went through its earlier stages under the Flavian emperors (AD 69–96), and reached the consulship in AD 97, the year which nearly saw a repetition of the bloody civil war which followed the death of Nero. Despite such a favoured career, however, Tacitus claims not to have been influenced by it in the matter of his historical judgements. It is usually assumed that in this he failed and that he used his career as a writer of history to denigrate individual emperors and the system of the principate in general.

Although Tacitus makes few personal statements in his works, just sufficient may be gathered from what he does say and from the apparent development of his writing career to hypothesise concerning his views of the material which he was handling. It is certainly clear from his biography of his father-in-law, Agricola, (published in AD 98) that he, like many senators, had found Domitian's reign difficult to bear. However, despite his clearly critical evaluation of that period, he did not assume that every emperor was necessarily similar to Domitian, nor, importantly, that the principate was a flawed institution. On the contrary, his remarks about Nerva (AD 96–8) and Trajan (AD 98–117) indicate that he saw in their reigns a resolution of difficulties that had in earlier reigns been painfully apparent. These difficulties centred around what Tacitus referred to as the long irreconcilability of 'principate' and 'liberty'. In this he recognised two problems: first, the *princeps* needed to be able to work with the senate without dominating its members; second, the position of *princeps* should be open to the aspirations of any senator. Nobody's expectations should be dimmed because they did not belong to a particular family. In other words, the greatest enemy of liberty was a *hereditary* monarchy and the arrogant and capricious rulers that resulted. This view is stated explicitly in an important oration which Tacitus put into the mouth of the emperor, Galba, in AD 69 (*Histories* I.15–16).

Having identified a problem, the development of Tacitus's writing career indicates his search for its solution; despite his stated intention of eventually writing a history of the reigns of Nerva and Trajan, Tacitus seems instead to have pushed his probing ever further back in time, with the ultimate realisation that to understand the principate he would need to fathom the policies and times of Augustus Caesar.

Tacitus was not, therefore, seeking to denigrate Tiberius and his government – indeed, in many aspects he clearly did not do so. Rather, he wished to examine Tiberius' reign to discover its contribution to the relationship between principate and liberty. Despite its many good qualities, the reign of Tiberius ultimately made a negative contribution, partly because Tiberius was the product of a dynastic system, and partly because, despite his obviously honourable intentions, the behaviour of the *princeps* was arbitrary; arbitrariness in government was a feature of domination (*dominatio*), not of principate.

In his study of Tiberius, Tacitus was aware of a damaging inconsistency in an emperor who pursued policies that were generally sound and fair, but who, particularly in his dealings with the senate, could create by his manner a far from favourable impression. It was desirable, therefore, that Tacitus' treatment should concentrate upon trying to expose this inconsistency and demonstrate its effects; it was for this reason that much of Tacitus' narrative was concentrated on the personal interaction of the *princeps* with those around him. By including rumour (for which he has often been castigated) and dramatically reconstructing the reactions of *princeps* and senators, reporting their words and thoughts, Tacitus attempted to demonstrate the interaction *as it happened*. Tacitus has often been accused of thereby making an action appear less favourable than he should have done. But in reality he demonstrated why senators found the words and actions of the *princeps*, which on the face of things might appear sound, not only damaging but even intimidating. It was essentially within the context of these personal encounters that Tiberius' failure seems to have occurred, and it was there that it had to be demonstrated; rumour very often conveyed the essence of an immediate – and significant – reaction.

The Tiberius whom Tacitus recorded was essentially the Tiberius as he was seen by his contemporaries. For example, in his treatment of Tiberius' dealings with Germanicus, Tacitus has often been accused of glorifying Germanicus to the detriment of Tiberius, and so blackening the *princeps*. In fact, Tacitus rightly recognised the fear and suspicion that dominated the relationship, but the glorification of Germanicus that is obvious in the narrative is a record of the *contemporary* glorification which helped to sour the relationship further and cause, for example, the rumours which proliferated around Germanicus' posting to the east in AD 17 and his subsequent death.

Tacitus recognised Tiberius' good qualities; his account was not constructed to denigrate the *princeps*, but to demonstrate through the highlighting of successive episodes how the gulf between principate and liberty, already harmed by the dynastic succession, deepened as a result of the inability of Tiberius and his contemporaries to relate to one another. The anxiety to do right and the simple modesty of the *princeps* were both lost sight of as the character of the reign deteriorated and men came to fear for their lives. On the whole, however, it was Tacitus' view that it was the blindness of the *princeps* which led to this; it was no act or intention of tyranny.

Tacitus rarely indicates the sources of his information, though the senatorial records (*acta senatus*) are generally reckoned to have been important to him. These will have contained records of debates and speeches, and from this source Tacitus may have drawn the items of vocabulary and phraseology that have been recognised as characteristically Tiberian. It is known that the Elder Pliny wrote an account of Rome's *German Wars* which will have provided information on the campaigning of Germanicus. Many of Tiberius' contemporaries wrote accounts of their lives, including the younger Agrippina, who, it may be assumed, was a rather tendentious source, though Tacitus does cite her for a detail concerning her mother. Tiberius, too, wrote his memoirs, and they are cited by Suetonius and known to have been read by the later emperor, Domitian (AD 81–96). Further, the works of 'serious' historians, such as Valerius Maximus, Aufidius Bassus, Servilius Nonianus, and the emperor Claudius, covered the period in question. That Tacitus will have consulted these is not in doubt; how he *used* them is far more speculative.

Suetonius' *Life of Tiberius* was published in the 120s, probably after the biographer's fall from favour in the early years of Hadrian's reign, and forms Book III of the *Lives of the Caesars*. Suetonius' career was different from that of Velleius and Tacitus in that he remained of equestrian status and did not enter the senate. Much of what we know of Suetonius is derived from references in the *Letters* of his friend and contemporary, the Younger Pliny.

For much of his life, Suetonius was a schoolmaster, following a profession which required an almost encyclopaedic knowledge, gained from the collection of examples of grammatical and rhetorical oddities which were the Roman schoolmaster's stock-in-trade. The mind of the compiler is always evident in Suetonius – both in the list of his published works and in the way in which he treated his individual subjects. Pliny's evidence shows Suetonius to have been a staid and rather fussy man who, because of his excessively superstitious nature, found it very difficult to act decisively. Yet, perhaps through the influence of Pliny, he eventually reached the important secretarial posts which he held under Trajan and Hadrian. These posts would not only have required the great thoroughness which his works and earlier career suggest, but would also have given great scope for research in the imperial archives which he was able to put to such good use. For example, his knowledge and use of Augustus' correspondence allowed him to demonstrate the reliance which Augustus placed upon Tiberius and even the affection that may have played its part in their relationship – something at which Velleius hinted but did little to prove, and which most contemporaries believed to be far from the truth.

Suetonius' access to his 'privileged' material came to an end in about AD 122 when, along with Septicius Clarus (the prefect of the praetorian guard), he was sacked by Hadrian. From what is said by Hadrian's biographer, Spartianus (in the *Writers of the Augustan History*), the cause of this would seem to have been a lapse in propriety rather than anything more serious. It is, however, apparent that once Suetonius was divorced from his source material, the standard of his writing deteriorated; his later imperial biographies are very sketchy by comparison with the first three.

Suetonius is often castigated on the irrelevant ground that he was not a historian; biography required a different perspective, in which the life of the subject was inevitably the dominant theme. After the manner of Roman orators, Suetonius displayed his subject by gathering material under various 'headings' without necessarily any attention to chronological development. Typical of such 'headings' (which are not of course explicitly indicated) are family history, omens preceding the birth of the subject, life prior to accession, reign, physical characteristics, death and relevant omens. Occasionally it may be hard to detect these 'headings' fully, as in the *Life of Caligula*, in which the only clear division is that between the acts of the *princeps* and those of the monster.

The *Life of Tiberius* is regarded as being amongst the biographies of better quality, probably researched whilst Suetonius still enjoyed privileged access to his material; for instance, the correspondence of Augustus is used to good effect to show a view of Augustus' relationship with Tiberius different from that normally accepted. We can see clear evidence of Suetonius' pleasure in compilation – in particular in his account of the previous history of the Claudian and Livian families and in his description of the perversions alleged to have characterised the retirement of the *princeps*. In general, however, despite the volume of information, Suetonius' account of Tiberius is not penetrative; its anecdotal approach tends to superficiality, and lacks the depth achieved by the rigorous analysis offered by Tacitus.

As is the case with the account of Dio Cassius, one of Suetonius' chief values is that of supplying gaps in our knowledge caused by the loss of portions of Tacitus' manuscript. As a sole source, however, for particular events, Suetonius' account carries considerable dangers for the modern historian; where he can be checked we observe a tendency to turn particular incidents, whatever the peculiar nature of their circumstances, into illustrations of general characteristics. As an example we may cite the observation that, during the reign of Tiberius, young virgins who were to be executed were first raped by the executioner; other evidence makes it clear that this observation was based upon an isolated incident – the execution of Sejanus' daughter, which was of course deeply embedded in special circumstances.

Thus, whilst Suetonius undoubtedly adds to the body of information available, he does not bear comparison with Tacitus in terms of his ability to analyse that information.

The *Roman History* of Dio Cassius was written approximately a century later than the works of Suetonius and Tacitus. Dio was an unusual figure in that his family was not only Greek but already of consular standing. He reached a first consulship around AD 205 and remained high in the favour of the Severans, although entertaining a clear distaste for some of the family – for example, the eminently uncongenial Caracalla. He reached a second consulship in AD 229, with the emperor Severus Alexander as his colleague, but died shortly afterwards.

Dio records clearly his reasons for writing the *Roman History*: having early on published an account of the signs portending Severus' rise to power, and having (not surprisingly) found the favour of the emperor for this, he turned as a result of his own inspiration and imperial prompting to write a full account of Roman history. Dio goes on to say that he spent ten years researching the material up to the death of Severus in AD 211 and a further twelve years putting it together.

We do not know precisely Dio's view of historiography, since his preface is now lost, but it would appear to encompass the aims of both entertaining and informing. His preoccupations were those of his class, he dwelt particularly on the effects of the principate and its institutions on the senatorial order, and was not concerned to elucidate the rapid social and economic developments witnessed across the Empire. Some of the thinking which depended upon the experiences of his own life and career was particularly appropriate to the early principate: he had seen the effects of disastrous dynastic arrangements, as Commodus succeeded Marcus Aurelius and as Caracalla succeeded his father, Septimius Severus. He was familiar also with an emperor (Septimius Severus) who promised respect for the corporate senate and security for its members and failed to keep the promise. He was aware of the contrast between the principate and the *respublica*, but not obsessed by it to the extent of regarding the former as a travesty of the latter.

Events had moved on through the first two centuries AD, so that men of Dio's day, as is shown by the long speech put into the mouth of Augustus' friend, Maecenas, in Book LII, appear to have been content with their monarch, so long as he was benevolent. Such a benevolence is clearly to be seen in Dio's famous report of Tiberius' objection to the title *dominus* ('lord'): 'I am lord to my slaves, general to the armies, and *princeps* to the senate.' Dio shared the view propounded by others in the second century AD that the Roman Empire was an almost ideal organisation in which everyone, great and small, was guaranteed due rights by the natural beneficent wisdom of the ruler. No mechanism is envisaged for either the education or the controlling of the emperor, though it has been suggested that Maecenas' speech may have been intended as an educative tract for the youthful Severus Alexander. It is significant that the experiences and times of Augustus may have been used for this purpose; similarly, Dio may have had in mind the gradualist approach of Augustus when he criticised the honourable and decent Pertinax (AD 192) for trying to put right too quickly the wrongs of Commodus' reign.

In institutional terms the principate had moved on from its foundation by Augustus, and it is not appropriate to see the military despotism of Severus in the same light as the principates of Augustus or of Tiberius. Similarly, much had changed in the detail of imperial administration. The Severan senate was not like that of the early principate; nor were the early distinctions between senators and equestrians still appropriate in the early third century AD. In view of this, it is inevitable that Dio should display anachronistic lapses.

Dio certainly believed that the writer of history should entertain. Like Tacitus, Dio tried to achieve the smoothly running narrative that would keep the attention of a listening audience, not one interrupted by citation of sources and references to the kinds of detail which would have rendered many episodes – particularly those of a military nature – more intelligible. Like Tacitus again, Dio set out to follow an annalistic framework, yet his interest in a 'story' frequently led him to ignore it, whereas Tacitus in his Tiberian books adhered to the framework almost without exception.

Finally, the effect of the predominance of rhetoric in education led to the enhancing beyond any reasonable verification of individual episodes, so as to make them dramatic, entertaining and worthy of Dio's theme. Rhetorical embellishment is to be seen also in the composition of speeches for historical personages. This, of course, had a long history in Graeco-Roman historiography, though Dio's efforts are freer compositions than those of most of his predecessors – not only in length but also in their use as vehicles for the historian's own thoughts.

Dio's account of Tiberius' reign is preserved in a very fragmentary form, and adds little of substance to what is available in Tacitus and Suetonius. However, he does provide a continuous source for the crucial two years prior to Sejanus' fall which are missing from the transmitted manuscript of Tacitus' *Annals*. In particular, he offers some clue to what may have lain behind Tiberius' turning on Sejanus. He also shows the lack of clarity that may have attached to the allegiances of various of the protagonists in the period preceding Sejanus' fall, when he reports Tiberius' complaint to Asinius Gallus over the latter's alleged interference in the relationship between Sejanus and the *princeps*. It is Dio too who reports upon elements of Tiberius' contingency planning in the months leading up to his denunciation of Sejanus. Although not all of this is clear, it does offer, as no other surviving account does, a basis for understanding the course of this momentous episode between AD 29 and 31.

In all, this varied source material allows us to trace the course of a reign which was bound to exhibit considerable strains due to Tiberius' personality and to the fact that he was the first successor to the principate of Augustus. The contribution of each of the four main sources is invaluable; without any of them there would be considerable impairment of our ability to understand the personality and principate of Tiberius Caesar.

Appendix II
The evidence of inscriptions and coins

Although the quantity of surviving inscriptions relating to the reigns of the early emperors is less impressive than for their later successors, some highly significant documents remain from the Julio-Claudian period. Many of these offer important information to put alongside that of the written sources for the life and principate of Tiberius.

Many record honours offered by loyal communities to various members of the imperial family, and in some cases the imperial replies are preserved. A particularly interesting one concerns an offer of divine honours for Augustus, Tiberius and Livia made by the civic leaders of Gytheum in Greece. In his reply Tiberius adopted an approach which is also evident in the written sources: no honour was too great for Augustus, whilst Tiberius himself was content with honours which were more moderate and befitting a mere human, and Livia would have to come to her own decision. This is paralleled in Tacitus' accounts of Tiberius' refusal of the request made by inhabitants of the province of Further Spain to be permitted to build a temple to him (*Annals* IV. 37–8), and of the attitude taken by Tiberius in a case in which insults were alleged to have been made against himself, Augustus and Livia (*Annals* II. 50).

The surviving cenotaph inscription for Gaius Caesar (in Pisa) referred to the cruelty of fate in words that echoed Augustus' own reference in his will to the loss, and indicates the depth of despair felt at a time when Augustus' dynastic policy appeared devastated. Inscriptions survive which give expansive information on the honours given to Germanicus and Drusus after their deaths, whilst a coin from Asia Minor indicates the apotheosis of these 'new gods of brotherly love'. Personal and public inscriptions show individuals and communities recording their vows for the continued health and safety of the *princeps* ('pro salute Ti. Caesaris'). Many, from all parts of the Empire, record the gratitude of communities to Tiberius for his encouragement and help in the erection of public buildings and services, showing that, whilst Tiberius was in no sense a prolific builder in Rome, his record in the provinces was far more impressive.

The hatred generated in the reign, however, is also demonstrated through the practice of erasing from public inscriptions the names of those who had fallen seriously from favour; among those from Tiberius' reign are (not surprisingly) Sejanus, Cnaeus Piso (*legatus* of Syria during Germanicus' eastern commission), and (posthumously) Tiberius himself. A number of inscriptions record the gratitude of individuals and communities for the punishing of Sejanus for his 'wicked plans', and one from Rome's Aventine Hill (the traditional home of the *plebs*) recalls an earlier attempt to arouse enthusiasm for Sejanus some months before his disgrace.

Perhaps the most enlightening and entertaining documents to have survived are papyrus fragments relating to Germanicus' visit to Egypt shortly before his death – a visit which occasioned severe criticism from the *princeps* (see Chapter 5, p. 38). First, a papyrus which appears to give an on-the-spot account of Germanicus' arrival in Alexandria offers confirmation of the informal, even histrionic, behaviour of the young man, which is evident in Tacitus' account of many of his actions during the mutiny amongst the Rhine legions. It also indicates that it had never occurred to Germanicus that his entry into Egypt, the private domain of the *princeps*, would be frowned upon: not only that, but his use of the Greek word equivalent to *provincia* ('province') shows that without thinking he treated Egypt as if it was a normal province covered by his command. Further, two other papyri carry the texts of edicts issued by Germanicus in Egypt, showing that he gave instructions which he thought necessary without referring to Tiberius. There is irony in the fact that Germanicus instructed the Egyptians not to afford him divine honours which would cause envy, without considering that it was his mere presence in Egypt that gave cause for offence.

The coinage of Tiberius' reign is not prolific in the variety of its issues, though many of them are extremely instructive. Commemorations of the deified Augustus are unremitting, which serves to confirm the picture given by the sources of the extreme respect always offered by Tiberius to his predecessor. Both Livia and Drusus also find prominent places on Tiberius' coinage.

However, some of the most striking issues are those concerned with events of the reign or with the qualities of Tiberius' principate. A series of personifications commemorate Justice (IVSTITIA), Augustan Health (SALVS AVGVSTA) and Piety (PIETAS), with busts on the obverse of the coins which may have used Livia as a 'model'. Two further 'virtues', *Clementia* and *Moderatio*, figure on reverse designs, and in all probability reflect Tiberius' own view of his treatment of treason cases in the senate in the early part of his reign.

Two issues commemorate the Temples of Vesta and Concord, which Tiberius was involved in rebuilding, though before he became *princeps*. The generosity of the *princeps* to the Asian cities following the earthquake of AD 17 is recorded. Finally, a fine and unusual design with the heads of two infants on the tops of crossed *cornucopiae* records the birth of twins to Drusus and Livilla.

In all, whilst there is not sufficient numismatic material to provide a documentation parallel to that of the written sources, clear evidence is given of the view which Tiberius took of his principate and of the ideas which were important to him.

Appendix III
Chief dates in the life of Tiberius

BC	44	Assassination of Julius Caesar (15 March)
	43	Formation of triumvirate between Octavian, Antony and Lepidus
	42	Battle of Philippi; deaths of Brutus and Cassius; birth of Tiberius (16 November)
	41	Perusine war
	39	Treaty of Misenum; return of Tiberius' family to Rome; Livia's divorce from Ti. Nero and marriage to Octavian
	38	Birth of Tiberius' brother, Nero Drusus
	32	Death of Ti. Nero
	31	Battle of Actium
	27	First settlement of the principate
	23	Second settlement of the principate
	22–21	Augustus and Tiberius win diplomatic settlement with Parthia
	16–7	Tiberius in Gaul and Germany
	13	First consulship of Tiberius
	12	Death of Agrippa; Tiberius required to divorce Vipsania and marry Julia
	9	Death of Nero Drusus in Germany
	7	Second consulship of Tiberius
	6	Tiberius given a grant of tribunician power (–1BC); retires to Rhodes

AD	2	Julia scandal; Tiberius required to divorce her
	2	Death of Gaius Caesar; Tiberius returns to Rome
	4	Death of Lucius Caesar; Augustus adopts Tiberius as his son (Tiberius Julius Caesar); Tiberius given grants of tribunician power and proconsular power
	6–9	Pannonian revolt
	7	Banishment of Agrippa Postumus and the younger Julia
	9	Varus disaster in Germany
	12	Tiberius given 'co-regency' with Augustus (?)
	14	Death of Augustus; accession of Tiberius; death of Agrippa Postumus; mutinies amongst the Rhine and Danube legions
	14–16	Germanicus' campaigns in Germany
	15	Sejanus becomes sole prefect of the praetorian guard
	17	Earthquake shatters cities in Asia Minor
	17–20	Germanicus' proconsular power in the east
	17–24	Rebellion of Tacfarinas in north Africa
	19	Death of Germanicus; birth of Drusus' twins
	20	Trial and suicide of Cnaeus Piso
	21	Tribunician power given to Drusus
	21–22	Rebellion of Sacrovir in Gaul
	23	Death of Drusus; concentration of the praetorian guard within Rome
	24	Opening of Sejanus' campaign against Agrippina, her friends and family
	26	Thracian insurrection
	26–27	Tiberius' decision to retire from Rome
	29	Prosecution of Agrippina, Nero, Drusus and Asinius Gallus; death of Livia
	30	Tiberius supposedly warned by Antonia concerning the true aims of Sejanus; suicide of Nero
	31	Joint consulship of Tiberius and Sejanus; denunciation and death of Sejanus (18 October)
	33	Financial crisis in Rome; deaths of Agrippina, Drusus and Asinius Gallus
	34–36	Death of Artaxias of Armenia, followed by resettlement of the east
	36	Fire on the Aventine Hill
	37	Suicide of Lucius Arruntius; death of Tiberius and accession of Gaius Caligula (16 March)

Appendix IV
Glossary of Latin terms

Auctoritas This concept, which was central to the Augustan principate, is hard to render precisely; it means 'influence' and 'prestige', and embraces the idea of acquiring these through a combination of heredity, personality and achievement. Importantly, it implies the ability to patronise on a large scale.

Clementia This means 'clemency', or being sparing to political adversaries: whilst it might on particular occasions be welcome in its effects, in principle it was a 'virtue' related to men of overwhelming (and, thus, unwelcome) power, which could be denied as capriciously as it was exercised.

Consul The *consul* was the head of the executive branch of government during the republic; two were elected each year, and were accountable to the electorate for their tenure of office. They presided over meetings of the senate and assemblies of the *populus* (whole people), and, until the late third century BC, regularly commanded the armies in battle, until this function was increasingly taken over by promagistrates (*proconsul*, *propraetor*). Under the principate, whilst prestige still attached to the office, its importance came to relate more to the provincial and army commands for which it represented a 'qualification'. Also under the principate it became normal for the consuls who took office on 1 January (*ordinarii*), and who gave their names to the year, to resign midway through the year in favour of replacements (*consules suffecti*). This was a method of increasing the numbers of men qualified for senior commands.

Cursus Honorum The ladder of office climbed during the republic by senators in their quest for the consulship; it was subject to a number of organising laws (e.g. the *Lex Villia* of 180 BC, and a *Lex Cornelia* of Sulla), which laid down intervals between offices as well as the proper order for holding them. Under the principate, the *cursus* remained in place, though a man's progress along it was affected by imperial favour (or the lack of it), and by the number of his legitimate children. The chief offices under the principate (and ages of tenure) were:

Office	Age
Vigintivirate (board of twenty)	18
Military tribune	21–2
Quaestor	25
Tribune of the plebs (often omitted)	
Aedile (often omitted)	
Praetor	30–5
Legionary commander (*legatus legionis*)	30+
Consul	37+
Proconsul or *legatus Augusti*	38+

Dignitas This 'dignity' referred specifically to the holding of offices of the *cursus honorum*. It was, for example, an affront to Caesar to be barred from competing for a second consulship, which by 50 BC he was entitled to do. Similarly, Tiberius took it as an affront to his *dignitas* that in 6 BC he was given tribunician power simply to annoy Gaius and Lucius Caesar.

Dominatio The state of being a master (*dominus*): the word originally and properly referred to the state of being a master of slaves, but is increasingly used to describe the position and behaviour of Julius Caesar and (by some) of Augustus.

Equites Members of the equestrian order were during the principate Rome's second social class. Originally a rather disparate body, the order acquired coherence through its commercial activities following the expansion of empire from the second century BC. Companies formed within the order (*societates*) undertook (for profit) many tasks during the republic of a civil service nature. Augustus re-organised the order so that it had a career structure in which it carried out similar tasks but for salaries rather than profits.

Imperium The executive *power* bestowed on consuls and praetors during the republic, through which they 'controlled' the state. *Imperium* was tenable as it was defined – consular, proconsular. Augustus under the first settlement controlled Gaul, Spain and Syria under a proconsular *imperium*, which was enhanced to superiority over others (*maius*) under the second settlement. He had a permanent 'residual' *imperium*, which could be temporarily redefined to enable him to undertake other tasks, such as censorial duties.

Legatus Originally a man to whom 'assistant' power was delegated; Pompey, for example, conducted his eastern campaigns with a number of *legati* in attendance. Under the principate, a man became a *legatus* of a legion after the praetorship, but the term was usually employed of those to whom the emperor delegated *de facto* control of his provinces (*legatus Augusti pro praetore*), where the term 'propraetore' was used by ex-consuls in order visibly to subordinate them to the emperor's proconsular *imperium*.

Lex A law, which has been passed either by one of the assemblies (*comitia*) of the whole people (*populus*), or by the assembly of the plebeians (*concilium plebis*). Under the principate, the participation of these bodies became a mere formality.

Libertas 'Freedom' had a wide collection of meanings in Rome, though that most frequently mentioned was the traditional *freedom* of the nobility to progress along the *cursus honorum* without undue interference from others. It was this *libertas* that was seen as being in conflict particularly with the principle of hereditary succession.

Nobilis Literally, one who was 'known'; the *nobiles* (aristocracy) defined themselves as deriving from families which had reached the consulship in earlier generations, and regarded the consulship as virtually their birthright.

Optimates The *optimates* (or self-styled 'best men') during the republic were those *nobiles* who felt that their factional dominance should be exercised primarily through an influential senate

91

taking the leading role in government. It was effectively the *optimates*, with their blinkered view of Rome and its Empire, who forced Caesar and Pompey to war in 49 BC, and who were instrumental in Caesar's assassination five years later. In the early principate they and their descendants found the family of the Claudii a more suitable rallying point than that of the Julii.

Patrician Traditionally the oldest part of Rome's aristocracy who in the republic's early days exercised the decisive role in government, maintaining a stranglehold through law and patronage over the political, military, legal and religious machinery of the state. The 'struggle of the orders' (traditionally 509–287 BC) gave more equality to *rich* plebeians, so that the real effectiveness of the distinction between the classes was eroded. Subsequently, the main factional groups (*optimates* and *populares*) each contained members of both classes. Augustus tried to revive the patriciate as the central core of his patronised aristocracy. Patricians were debarred from holding plebeian offices, such as the tribunate of the plebs and the plebeian aedileship.

Pietas The 'sense of duty' to gods, state and family that represented the traditional loyalties of the Roman noble, and which Augustus tried to exemplify and revitalise.

Populares The term, meaning 'mob-panderer', was coined by the *optimates* to describe the way in which their opponents appeared to devalue the senate's role in government, and to place their emphasis on manipulating the popular assemblies. The first notable *popularis* was Ti. Sempronius Gracchus (tribune of the plebs in 133 BC). Although the term fell into disuse after the republic, nobles of this view tended to identify with the Julian family of Augustus, perhaps reflecting Caesar's position of primacy amongst the *populares* in the 50s and 40s BC.

Praefectus Under the principate, the term 'prefect' was applied to various grades within the reformed equestrian order, from the commands of auxiliary army units to some of the highest officers in the order (*praefecti* of Egypt and of the praetorian guard).

Praetor This was the office second in importance to the consulship, although the praetors may in the earliest days have been the chief magistrates – *prae-itor* meaning 'one who goes in front'. From Sulla's time they had an increasing importance as the presiding officers in the courts (*quaestiones*); the post led on to legionary commands and/or governorships of second-rank provinces.

Princeps The term 'chief man' was favoured by Augustus as a form of address; it did not imply a particular office, but throughout the republic had been applied to those who, in or out of office, were deemed to be prestigious, influential and disposers of patronage.

Princeps senatus A republican term applied to the man who in terms of seniority (however conceived) was placed at the head of the list of senators, as Augustus was after the *lectio senatus* of 28 BC.

Proconsul The term was originally applied to a consul whose *imperium* had been extended beyond his term of office as consul to enable him to continue command of an army; by the second century BC, it was regularly applied to those who commanded provinces after their year of office in Rome: during the principate it was used of the governors (whether ex-consuls or ex-praetors) of senatorial provinces.

Procurator The term was used of various grades of equestrian in the emperor's financial service – from the chief agents in the provinces, down to quite minor officials in their departments. They were officially distinguished by an adjective describing their different salary levels.

Respublica This word, often used emotively to describe the nature of the state which Augustus supplanted after Actium, means simply 'the public concern'. By definition, therefore, it would be negated by anyone with overwhelming and capriciously exercised power (*dominatio*).

Senatus consultum The decree issued at the end of a senatorial debate which was not *legally* binding, but an advisory statement passing on the senate's opinion to those popular bodies responsible for making the final decisions and passing laws.

Tribune of the plebs Originally appointed, according to tradition in 494 BC, the tribunes were officers charged with defending their fellow plebeians against injustices perpetrated by patricians. The decisive elements in their 'armoury' were the 'veto', by which they could bring any business (except that of a dictator) to a halt, and the 'sacrosanctity', by which all plebeians were bound by oath to defend an injured or wronged tribune. Gradually, the tribunes were drawn into the regular business of office-holding – almost, but not quite, part of the *cursus honorum*; their veto was employed increasingly as a *factional* weapon, and they became potentially powerful through their ability to legislate with the plebeian assembly without prior consultation with the senate. Under the principate, little of their power remained, dominated as it was by the emperor's tribunician power (*tribunicia potestas*). Augustus, because he was by adoption a patrician, could not hold the office of tribune, though between 36 and 23 BC, he acquired most of the powers of the office, and outwardly used them as the basis of his conduct of government in Rome. The power served to stress his patronage and protection of all plebeians.

Triumvirate   Any group of *three* men; the first triumvirate of 60 BC was the informal arrangement for mutual assistance between Pompey, Crassus and Caesar; the second triumvirate of 43 BC was the legally based 'office' of Octavian, Antony and Lepidus. The term continued to be used of occasional groups of three, and regularly of the three mint officials (*triumviri* (or *tresviri*) *monetales*) and the punishment officials (*triumviri* (or *tresviri*) *capitales*), both of which groups were sections of the board of twenty, or vigintivirate, the first posts on the senatorial *cursus honorum*.

Bibliography

Abbreviations

AJP   *American Journal of Philology*
Cl. Phil *Classical Philology*
G & R   *Greece and Rome*
JRS   *Journal of Roman Studies*
TAPA   *Transactions of the American Philological Association*

Primary source material

The chief ancient literary sources for Tiberius' reign have all been translated into English:

Dio Cassius, *Roman History*, Books LVI–LVII, translated by E. Cary (Loeb Classical Library)
Suetonius, *The Twelve Caesars (Lives of the Caesars)*, translated by Robert Graves (Penguin Classics)
Tacitus, *The Annals of Imperial Rome*, Books I–VI, translated by M. Grant (Penguin Classics)
Velleius Paterculus, *Roman History*, Book II, 87–131, translated by F. W. Shipley (Loeb Classical Library)

The evidence of contemporary coins is discussed in:

C. H. V. Sutherland, *Coinage in Roman Imperial Policy, 31* BC–AD 68, London 1951

C. H. V. Sutherland, *The Roman Imperial Coinage*, Vol.I (revised edition, London 1984)

Collections of relevant inscriptions are available in:

V. Ehrenberg and A. H. M. Jones, *Documents Illustrating the Reigns of Augustus and Tiberius*, Oxford 1955

S. J. Miller, *Inscriptions of the Roman Empire, AD 14–117* (Lactor No.8, London Association of Classical Teachers)

Secondary material

The reign of Tiberius, and particularly Tacitus' treatment of it, has prompted an exceptionally large bibliography, of which a selection is given below. The best surveys which treat Tiberius within the context of the early principate are:

Cambridge Ancient History, Vol X, Cambridge 1952
A. Garzetti, *From Tiberius to the Antonines*, London 1974

More specialised treatments are:

J. P. Balsdon, *The Emperor Gaius (Caligula)*, Oxford 1934

H. E. Bird, 'Aelius Sejanus and his Political Significance', *Latomus* XXVIII (1969), 85

A. Boddington, 'Sejanus. Whose Conspiracy?', *AJP* LXXXIV (1963), 1

C. W. Chilton, 'The Roman Law of Treason under the Early Principate', *JRS* XLV (1955), 73

M. Grant, *Aspects of the Principate of Tiberius*, New York 1950

M. Guido, *Southern Italy: An Archaeological Guide*, London 1972

M. Hammond, *The Augustan Principate*, New York 1933

A. H. M. Jones, *Augustus*, London 1970

B. Levick, 'Drusus Caesar and the Adoptions of AD 4', *Latomus* XXV (1966), 227

B. Levick, 'Julians and Claudians', *G & R* XXII (1975), 29

B. Levick, *Tiberius the Politician*, London 1976

G. Maranon, *Tiberius: A Study in Resentment*, London 1956

F. B. Marsh, 'Tacitus and Aristocratic Tradition', *Cl. Phil* XXI (1926), 289

F. B. Marsh, *The Reign of Tiberius*, Oxford 1931

J. Nicols, 'Antonia and Sejanus', *Historia* XXIV (1975), 48

A. E. Pappano, 'Agrippa Postumus', *Cl. Phil* XXXVI (1941), 30

C. Rodewald, *Money in the Age of Tiberius*, Manchester 1976

R. S. Rogers, 'The Conspiracy of Agrippina', *TAPA* LXII (1931), 141

R. S. Rogers, *Criminal Trials and Criminal Legislation under Tiberius*, Middletown 1935

R. S. Rogers, *Studies in the Reign of Tiberius*, Baltimore 1943

R. Seager, *Tiberius*, London 1972

R. Sealey, 'The Political Attachments of L. Aelius Sejanus', *Phoenix* XV (1961), 97.

D. C. A. Shotter, 'The Trial of Gaius Silius' (AD 24), *Latomus* XXVI (1967), 712

D. C. A. Shotter, 'Tacitus, Tiberius and Germanicus', *Historia* XVII (1968), 194

D. C. A. Shotter, 'Tiberius and Asinius Gallus', *Historia* XX (1971), 443

D. C. A. Shotter, 'Julians, Claudians and the Accession of Tiberius', *Latomus* XXX (1971), 1117

D. C. A. Shotter, 'Cnaeus Calpurnius Piso, Legate of Syria', *Historia* XXIII (1974), 229

D. C. A. Shotter, 'Cn Cornelius Cinna Magnus and the Adoption of Tiberius', *Latomus* XXXIII (1974), 306

D. C. A. Shotter, 'Tacitus and Tiberius', *Ancient Society* XIX (1988), 225

G. V. Sumner, 'The Family Connections of Lucius Aelius Sejanus', *Phoenix* XV (1961), 97

R. Syme, *The Roman Revolution*, Oxford 1939

R. Syme, *Tacitus*, Oxford 1958

R. Syme, 'History or Biography: The Case of Tiberius Caesar', *Historia* XXIII (1974), 481

L. R. Taylor, 'Tiberius' Refusal of Divine Honours', *TAPA* LX (1929), 8

B. Walker, *The Annals of Tacitus*, Manchester 1952

A. Wallace-Hadrill, *Suetonius: The Scholar and His Caesars*, London 1983

K. Wellesley, 'The *Dies Imperii* of Tiberius', *JRS* LVII (1967), 23

C. M. Wells, *The German Policy of Augustus*, Oxford 1972

Ch. Wirszubski, *Libertas as a Political Idea at Rome*, Cambridge 1950

Z. Yavetz, *Plebs and Princeps*, Oxford 1969